PROLOGUE

CW01500262

I have a confession to make. For over 40 years, I've been dealing with an obsession. In medical circles, obsessions are often labelled as persistent or recurring unwanted thoughts which intrude into daily life and cause significant distress. In contrast, my personal obsession, while time-consuming, has been a source of pleasure and joy over many years. It's called genealogy: the study of family history.

Let me tell you why it's so important in my life and how it all started.

In February 1981, my wife, Maggie, and I – along with our newborn son, Stephen – were living in a beautiful, 100-year-old cottage on the outskirts of Wexford. The cottage boasted three-feet-thick stone walls and lovely views of the lush green surrounding countryside. I was employed as a young doctor in the local hospital. Our lives were very happy – and very busy.

When our home phone rang one evening, I anticipated that the call would be from the hospital or from one of Stephen's proud grandparents. I was wrong, on both counts. A lovely lady introduced herself as Olive Dawson née Kennedy. She lived in Wexford with her husband, Barry, and five children. She told me that she was my second cousin. I was ashamed to admit to her that I barely knew all my Kennedy aunts and uncles (there are 10 of them), only some of my first cousins (31 in total, I now know) and none of my second cousins. Olive finished the call by saying that she would help me to learn more. She was true to her word.

A week later, we visited her home for a delightful dinner. We were joined by her aunt, Sr Barbara Kennedy, a Catholic nun in Bunclody, Co. Wexford and an expert in the family history of my Kennedy clan. She entertained us with lots of stories of her childhood growing up in Eglish, a rural townland near the town of Borrisokane in north Co. Tipperary. Near the end of dinner, Sr Barbara presented me with a beautifully hand-drawn family tree, along with the names of my great-grandparents and a depiction of many of their descendants.

BALLYBUNION

TO THE RIVER

**An Irishman's Story
of Survival on the
Death Railway**

KWAI

FERGUS KENNEDY is a retired family doctor with a lifelong passion for history. He was born and raised in Waterford and received his medical degree from University College Dublin in 1977. He emigrated to Canada in 1982, and for over thirty years has lived on Vancouver Island with his wife and family. He has been researching his father's experiences as a prisoner of war in Singapore and Thailand throughout his adult life.

BALLYBUNION
TO THE RIVER
KWAI

An Irishman's Story
of Survival on the
Death Railway

FERGUS KENNEDY

Gill Books

Gill Books
Hume Avenue
Park West
Dublin 12
www.gillbooks.ie

Gill Books is an imprint of M.H. Gill and Co.

© Fergus Kennedy 2025

978 18045 8332 6

Designed and typeset by Padraig McCormack
Edited by Noel O Regan
Proofread by Jane Rogers
Maps by Aux1 Design
Printed and bound in Great Britain by Clays Ltd, Elcograf S.p.A.
This book is typeset in 12.5 on 19pt, Adobe Garamond Pro

*The paper used in this book comes from the
wood pulp of sustainably managed forests.*

*To the best of our knowledge, this book complies in full with the requirements
of the General Product Safety Regulation (GPSR). For further information
and help with any safety queries, please contact us at productsafety@gill.ie*

A CIP catalogue record for this book is available from the British Library.

5 4 3 2 1

To Maggie, our children and grandchildren,
and the generations yet to come.

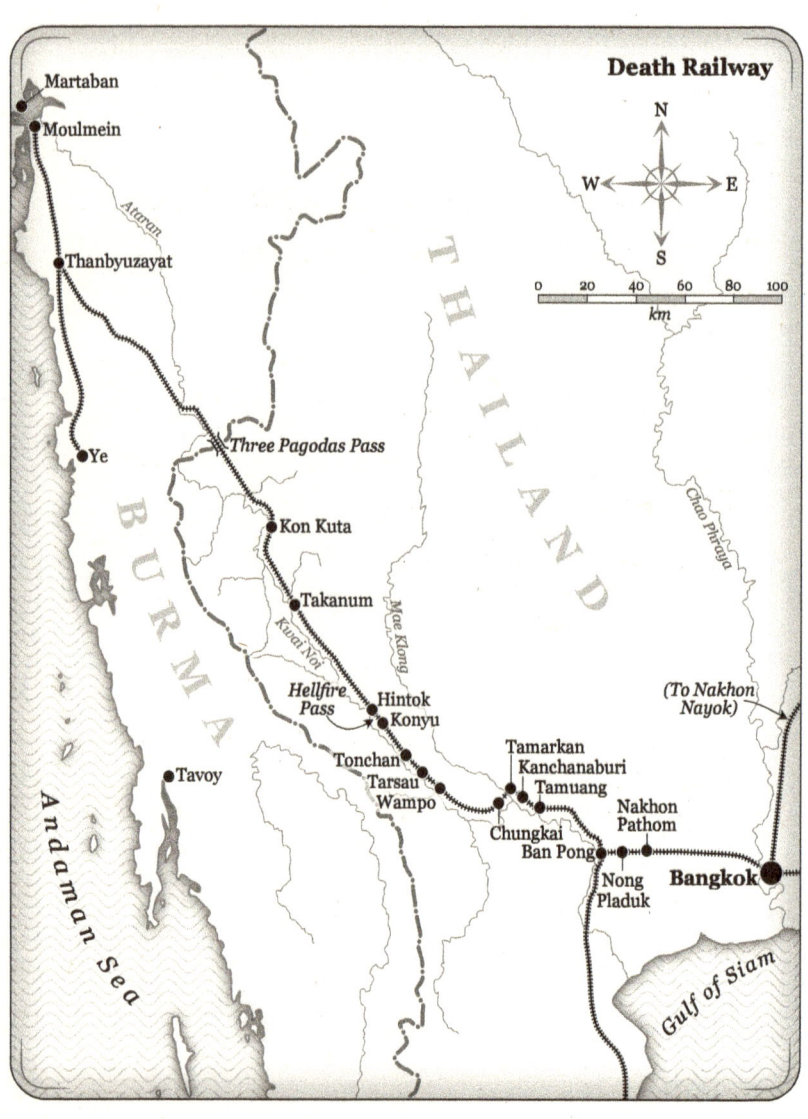

CONTENTS

PROLOGUE 9

01 Early Days 17

02 The Impregnable Fortress 26

03 The Death Railway 49

04 Slave Labour 63

05 Dead or Alive? 80

06 Speedo-Worko 86

07 Cholera 103

08 Miracle 124

09 The Red Cross and the 'V' Organisation 133

10 Weary Dunlop 144

11 Another Christmas in Captivity 158

12 Monotony 165

13 Farewell to the Jungle 177

14 Hell Ships 184

15 Friendly Fire 193

16 Goodbye to the Kwai 212

17 A Narrow Escape 220

18 Homecoming   229

19 Human Impact of the Death Railway   245

20 Married Life   250

EPILOGUE   264

BIBLIOGRAPHY   274

ACKNOWLEDGEMENTS   280

I was determined to know more and so began researching. Soon I learned that the original Kennedy (Cinnéide in Irish) was the father of Brian Boru, the famous High King of Ireland who defeated Viking invaders in the Battle of Clontarf in 1014. This and many other discoveries were pleasing and exciting to me. Many of the skills involved in family research were also appealing. For example, I had always enjoyed working out puzzles, ever since my father had taught me how to do cryptic crosswords as a boy. In school, I had loved learning about history and studying maps. In medicine, I enjoyed the art of differential diagnosis – that is, considering multiple possibilities and carefully analysing data to arrive at the right conclusion. These talents, it seemed to me, were at the heart of genealogy. As a result, I was hooked.

We emigrated to Alberta, Canada in 1982; however, if anything, my passion for family history only increased, as Maggie and I both wanted to ensure that our children did not lose their Irish roots. Stephen was joined by Deirdre in 1983, Aisling in 1985 and Mary Clare in 1987. We made sure to return to Ireland for family holidays as often as we could. On each of these visits, I would try to set aside a day in Dublin to search for family records. This involved visits to reading rooms in the National Archives,

General Register Office, National Library, Royal Irish Academy or Trinity College Library. Later, I found even more information by meeting and corresponding with relatives interested in family history. There seems to be one keen genealogist in each clan. It was wonderful to share knowledge with like-minded enthusiasts. The arrival of the internet, and, later, of affordable DNA testing, made searching even easier.

After 40 years, I now have a large family tree, depicting both my roots and Maggie's Gleeson ancestry. In total, there are over seventy thousand names. However, as time has passed, I've come to realise that I'm now less focused on expanding that family tree and much more interested in *family history.*

Each individual in the tree has a life story. Almost all will have had some drama worth retelling, and a few of them are as dramatic as a Hollywood movie. However, I will leave that task to other family historians; instead, I've decided to focus on a single unforgettable story, one which is close to my heart.

Just before the start of World War 2, my parents met and fell in love in the beautiful seaside town of Ballybunion, Co. Kerry, in the south-west corner of Ireland. Within a year, they were engaged and expected to marry soon after. They were wrong. Because of the war, they became separated by many thousands of miles for over five years. For most of that time, my mother did not know if her fiancé was alive or dead. Though he was a citizen of a neutral country, my father had become a prisoner of war (POW) of the Japanese empire. In fact, he was a slave labourer working on a railway running from Burma (modern-day Myanmar) to Thailand. The railway is now better known as the River Kwai Railway, or, more ominously, 'the Death Railway'. During this period, he endured conditions of cruelty and deprivation that are almost unimaginable, narrowly escaping death on several occasions. His incredible survival personifies courage, love, faith and tenacity in the midst of a prolonged nightmare – as well as some good luck. Luck that, incredibly, brings us back to Ballybunion.

This amazing story has not been easy to compile. My father, like many men from that era, did not like to talk about his war experiences and thought that silence was the best coping mechanism. If any of my six siblings or I asked him about those days, he, or my mother, would nearly always change the subject. Luckily, he did break his silence with me on rare occasions.

I remember watching the Oscar-winning film *The Bridge on the River Kwai* with him one Christmas when I was a boy. Afterwards, he told me that the Hollywood story was quite inaccurate, but he didn't explain further. Similarly, on another occasion we watched a movie about an attempted escape from a German POW camp. Afterwards, he told me how barbed wire fences had been unnecessary on the River Kwai; if a prisoner escaped, he would either die in the jungle or be easily recognisable to the local population, who would return him to the Japanese for a reward.

He did, of course, share all his wartime experiences with my mother. While he was alive, she honoured his wish not to talk about them with anyone else. In hindsight, I believe that she was simply trying to protect his mental health. She saw up close the nightmares that had plagued him for many years after the war and did not want to rekindle them. The term PTSD (post-traumatic stress disorder) had not yet come into common usage. However, after his death in 1989, my mother provided me with a treasure trove of stories.

My parents were not my only source of information. I read many books and memoirs about the experiences of POWs in Asia, especially on the River Kwai. I also came across insights through more serendipitous means. In 1991, our family moved from Alberta to the small town of Ladysmith on Vancouver Island, where I soon had a busy family practice. During this time, I became friendly with Dr Patricia 'Paddy' Mark, a family doctor in nearby Nanaimo. I was pleasantly surprised to learn that her father, originally from Northern Ireland, had worked as a medical officer on the River Kwai, and she willingly shared many of his personal memories with me.

In the early 2000s, an older man named Jack Farr became my patient. He soon told me that he had been a young pilot in the Royal Canadian Air Force (RCAF) based in India in World War 2. During the last two years of the war, he and his colleagues became known as the Burma Bombers. He had personally flown combat missions over the Burma–Thailand Railway, and one of his Canadian friends had even been the one to destroy the real 'Bridge on the River Kwai'. We spent a lot of time in my office chatting about his wartime experiences instead of his medical concerns.

By 2007, Maggie was a professor of nursing at Vancouver Island University (VIU) in Nanaimo. She and a colleague, Anna Grieve, were invited to present at a conference in Bangkok, Thailand, and kindly brought their husbands along for the trip. After the conference, we were able to arrange a minibus trip to Kanchanaburi, about 150km north-east of Bangkok, the site of the famous 'Bridge on the River Kwai'. Not only were we able to walk across the bridge, but we rode the railway over the raised wooden Wampo (Wang Pho) viaduct that my father had helped to build. It was an overwhelming experience and a day I will never forget.

A couple of years later, I learned that the British National Archives in Kew, London was releasing military records of POWs of the Japanese for the first time. My sister Irene, who lives in London, kindly agreed to go to Kew to look for our dad's records. Armed with only his military number, she soon held in her hands his British record written in his own handwriting, as well as a corresponding record in Japanese. Astonished, she emailed copies to me. I was incredulous. My father had provided me with a roadmap and exact timeline of his imprisonment – what a gift.

In 2022, my great-niece Sadhbh Murphy decided to write a high school history paper about my father's wartime story. She interviewed me at length for her project, amazed to learn how much information I had gathered.

'You should write a book,' Sadhbh told me.

I thought about it and realised that she was right; this remarkable family story deserves to be preserved for future generations. I hope you agree.

01 EARLY DAYS

By most standards, my parents had an exceptionally long engagement. Their romance began in the summer of 1939 in Ballybunion, Co. Kerry, and they became engaged in early 1940. At the time, they were unaware that it would be six agonising years before they could marry.

That summer of 1939 is remembered in Ireland and Britain as being unusually warm and sunny. Unfortunately, at the same time many people recognised that war in Europe was increasingly likely, as Hitler's Germany continued to threaten its neighbouring countries.

My father, Don Kennedy, then aged 25, was studying accountancy in University College Dublin (UCD). His best friend in college was Jim Trainor. Jim had the luxury of owning a somewhat antiquated car and, one weekend, invited a few male friends, including my dad, to accompany him on a trip to Ballybunion. By coincidence, my mother, Nora Ring – then aged 21, also attending UCD, but living in her family home in Mallow, Co. Cork during the summer holidays – did the same thing with a group of girlfriends. The two groups met and spent much of the weekend together.

Ballybunion is a popular seaside resort in north Kerry, famous for its world-renowned golf course, seaweed baths (said to have medicinal properties), clifftop walks with spectacular views, and several beaches. The two main beaches are known locally as 'ladies' beach' and 'men's beach'. They are so named because, in the distant past, only the respective genders were allowed to use each beach. (Presumably children swam with their mothers?) This separation of the sexes was ordered by the local parish priest, who walked by daily to ensure the rule wasn't broken. I imagine that this rule was no longer in place in 1939.

The attraction between the tall Dubliner and the petite Corkwoman was immediate, and sparks continued to fly over the next couple of days. At the end of the weekend, he asked her if they could continue dating when they returned to UCD. She agreed – on one condition.

In those days, UCD was a relatively small university situated in a single building in Earlsfort Terrace. This meant that most students knew each other and knew who was seeing a member of the opposite sex. As a result, Nora knew that Don had been courting another young woman back in Dublin, so her condition was that he would end that relationship as soon as he got back home. He instantly agreed and their romance blossomed when university restarted.

In many respects, their relationship was an unlikely one. He was from the capital city; she was from a small country town. He came from a large family with 10 siblings; she came from a single-parent family with only a single sister, Kathleen (usually known as Kay). Don had always lived at home; Nora, from the age of 10 onwards, spent most of the year away at school, first in Loreto Convent, Dalkey and then at UCD.

However, there were also similarities in their backgrounds. Both families were religious, with a strong Catholic faith. Don had two brothers, Dick and Paddy, both of whom were Jesuit priests, and a sister, Rene, who was a Loreto nun. The heads of both households, Don's father and Nora's mother, were strong-minded individuals who were successful in their chosen fields and were firm proponents of education for their children.

Their personalities were also alike. Both were outgoing and sociable with a wide circle of friends. Both were excellent athletes: Nora was captain of the UCD field hockey team and a good golfer; Don was a competitive runner and played rugby for Old Belvedere. Many of their traits may well have come from their parents.

Don Kennedy, 1935

Nora's parents were Denis Ring and Mary Healy. They married in 1912 and soon after he established a busy drapery store in West End, Mallow. Kathleen was born in 1913 and Nora in November 1917. Six months later, disaster struck: Denis was diagnosed with diabetes, for which there was no treatment at the time (insulin was discovered three years later). Because of the high sugar levels in his body, he developed an insatiable thirst. Friends and family went to a spa in Mallow to bring him buckets of water, as the water was reputed to have curative properties. It did not work. Within three weeks, Denis was dead and Mary was a young widow responsible for two young daughters and a small business.

She had no experience of running a business, but she was determined and a quick learner. Once or twice a year she would travel to London with her brother Jeremiah (who had a drapery in Kanturk) to keep up with the latest fashion trends. On rare occasions, she was even able to bring Kathleen or Nora (but not both) on the trip as a special treat. She was also a natural at engaging with her customers. For example, she was knowledgeable about sports (which impressed her male customers) and politics. She hated Éamon de Valera, and was not shy about saying so. As a result of her hard work, the drapery continued to thrive.

She continued to run the business until her early eighties, selling it to the business tycoon Ben Dunne in the late 1950s. Typically, she completed the deal without using any intermediaries. Dunnes Stores in Mallow remained at the West End location for the next 50 years. Mary lived to be 92. I am sure my mother inherited many of her personality traits, especially a feisty determination and a love of sports.

Don's parents were Denis Kennedy, a surgeon at St Vincent's Hospital in Dublin, originally from Eglish, North Tipperary, and Mary Langan, originally from Rathfeigh, Co. Meath. They married in 1900 and went on to have 11 children – six girls and five boys. Unusually for the time, all of them survived into adulthood. My father and his four older brothers attended Belvedere College, travelling up and down on the train each day from their home, a large house and estate called Hollywood, in Carrickmines.

Denis had a reputation for kindness with his patients but strictness in the operating room and at home. His nickname was 'Butcher Kennedy'. (I've been assured that this was a term of affection and not intended to be derogatory.) On one occasion, one of his daughters went out on a date. Her escort was given a strict deadline for her return home. When he missed the deadline by five minutes, Denis told the unfortunate suitor that he would never date her again. He never did.

His wife Mary, in contrast, was a warm, loving support for all her children. She herself was one of ten children who grew up on a farm in Co. Meath, so caring for her own large family seemed to come easily to her. She even found time to have her own small farming operation, with chickens, eggs, fruit and vegetables. These were sold locally, providing her with some extra income, which, we will shortly see, was a key factor in Don and Nora's love story.

Denis was proud that so many of his children became doctors (five: Kathleen, Leo, Dermot, Eileen and Maeve) or dedicated their lives to religious service (three: Dick, Paddy and Rene). He fully expected that Don would also go into medical school, so when Don opted for accountancy instead, the old man refused to speak to him for several months. Eventually, his mother – to whom Don was very close – acted as a mediator and peace was restored. Part of his reason for refusing medical school was that Don was squeamish about medical matters. Little did he realise that, within a few years, he would be exposed to some of the worst imaginable medical horrors.

———

The romance between Don and Nora became stronger in late 1939 and early 1940 – to the point where Don invited her to meet his parents. Nora was extremely nervous, but passed the test with flying colours, thereafter becoming a popular and frequent visitor to Don's home in Carrickmines.

During this time, as many had feared, war was declared in Europe. De Valera, who was now Taoiseach, decided that the country would remain neutral in the conflict. The USA also declared itself neutral, although it was providing material support to Britain through its 'Lend-Lease' agreement. The material, including food, oil and ships, was supplied at no initial charge, with the costs of the loan to be repaid over time when the war ended. Meanwhile, in the Pacific, an increasingly belligerent Japan was threatening the US and Britain with military action.

In the spring of 1940, Don successfully passed his accountancy exams and completed his practical experience at a large accountancy company in Dublin (Craig Gardiner and Co.). He knew that Nora was the love of his life and that he wanted to marry her. There was only one problem – he was broke. So he went to the other woman he loved, borrowing the money for an engagement ring from his mother.

Nora was delighted to accept his proposal of marriage. Now there was a new problem: unemployment. Due to 'the Emergency' – the state of emergency declared in Ireland throughout World War 2 – and the ongoing recession, there were no professional job openings in Ireland.

A friend and fellow accountant, John Bernard 'Barney' Byrne, told him about employment opportunities in the British Civil Service overseas, explaining how he was going to Hong Kong. Desperate, Don applied and was ultimately appointed to a position in Singapore, then part of Malaya. He was expected to start his new post in the summer of 1940.

Relieved, he and Nora decided that he would get established in Malaya and that she would join him the following year, whereupon they would marry in Singapore.

If only it had been that easy.

02 THE IMPREGNABLE FORTRESS

SINGAPORE, 1940-1942

Don sailed from Liverpool to Port Swettenham (now Port Klang) in Malaya on 3 July 1940, having first sailed from Dún Laoghaire to Holyhead in North Wales. He travelled on the SS *Eurybates* of the Blue Funnel Line. This was not a luxury liner – it was essentially a cargo ship with a few berths for private travellers (four in total on this voyage). By this time, the long voyage was very dangerous. Hitler's German forces had defeated France in June 1940. This enabled his submarines to use French ports as a base to attack British ships in the Atlantic Ocean, while his air force endangered ships in the Mediterranean Sea. As a result, the *Eurybates* was forced to avoid the Suez Canal and sail around Africa, adding weeks to the journey, which took about seven weeks in total.

Thankfully, Don arrived safely in Port Swettenham, after which he travelled overland down the Malay Peninsula to the island of Singapore to begin his career in the Malayan British Civil Service. He did well and soon became popular with his fellow workers and superiors. Finally, he was earning a good salary and was able to save some money. He also liked the tropical climate and the exotic cuisine. While there was persistent talk about possible Japanese aggression, he felt that this was unlikely to affect Malaya. He only saw positives for his future here. He and his fiancée could marry, have a good lifestyle and start a family. With this in mind, in late 1940 he sent word for Nora to join him in Singapore.

Despite the danger, she reserved passage to sail. I still have the passport issued to her in January 1941 – signed by her mother's least favourite politician, de Valera. However, by the time she received her passport, the danger to shipping from German submarines was even worse, resulting in the British government banning all sea travel for women and children. Consequently, Nora and Don's separation continued.

In fact, in the first half of 1941, the British government was not just concerned about nearby seas; they

Nora's passport

were worried for the safety of the furthest reaches of their empire. In May 1941, the British authorities were increasingly worried about a Japanese invasion of Malaya and other British territories in Asia. While Japan was not formally at war yet, it was part of a military pact with Germany and Italy (the Axis Forces). If it went to war, the Malayan rubber plantations and tin mines would be an invaluable source of raw material for its armed forces. To help fend off this threat, it was therefore decided that all British civil servants would be conscripted into the Federated Malay States Volunteer Force (FMSVF).

Don refused to be conscripted, pointing out that he was a citizen of a neutral country. The officer he spoke with was irate and put him in jail overnight for his disobedience. The next day, after receiving Don's Irish passport, the officer reluctantly agreed to release him. Once freed, however, my father immediately volunteered for the force.

I've often reflected on this sequence of events. Why did Don act as he did? I think he was determined to prove a point. He was a proud Irishman and, as he argued, a citizen of an independent, neutral country. Once the British authorities accepted that fact, he was prepared to fight the evil of the Japanese and German empires. I believe that these attributes of determination and courage would prove critical to his survival in the years to come.

He was trained to be a gunner. This involved operating large, fixed guns located at the south end of Singapore island, facing out to sea, as the authorities anticipated that this was how the Japanese would invade. How wrong they were.

———

On 8 December 1941 – or 7 December 1941 on the US mainland – the Japanese launched a sneak attack on the US Pacific Fleet at Pearl Harbor in Hawaii, declaring war on Britain and the USA after the attack was completed. At almost the same time, Japan launched troop invasions in north-east Malaya, Thailand and the Philippines.

The military campaign in defence of Malaya was a disaster for the Allied forces, despite outnumbering the Japanese two to one. Reasons for their capitulation included that few of the defensive units had been trained in jungle warfare and that they were often led by inexperienced British officers. Furthermore, the Japanese landing force had 57 tanks; the British had none. The Japanese also had air superiority. This advantage was compounded in the first days of the campaign when the

Allies retreated, leaving behind three intact northern airfields, which the Japanese soon put to good use as a base for their fighter and bomber planes.

When the invasion began, a new battleship, HMS *Prince of Wales*, and an old battlecruiser, HMS *Repulse*, had sailed north from Singapore to reinforce the British defences. On 10 December 1942, they were attacked by Japanese torpedobombers and both were sunk within two hours. This was devastating to British morale and their illusions of naval supremacy. When Winston Churchill was informed of the news, he wrote: 'In all the war, I never received a more direct shock.'

Back on land, the Allied troops continued to retreat, laden down with packs, blankets, gas masks and bulky canned rations. In contrast, the Japanese soldiers carried lightweight weapons and survived on a few handfuls of rice with some seaweed and pickles. They also used abandoned cars, trucks and even bicycles to increase their mobility, enabling them to repeatedly outflank their opposition. In addition, commandeered fishing boats were used to land seaborne units on the coast behind British lines, causing even more panic and bewilderment.

As they fled, the Allied officers looked for a better defensive position. They never found it. By 15 January 1942, the Japanese were only 100 miles north of

Singapore. Fierce fighting ensued for the next two weeks. Finally, the Japanese breached one part of the defensive line, putting the Allied soldiers at risk of encirclement. Once again, they were ordered to retreat.

In less than two months, the Japanese had reached the southern tip of the Malay peninsula. The retreating British and Australian forces crossed into Singapore on 31 January 1942, destroying part of the connecting 1,100-yard causeway behind them. This left at its narrowest point a mere 60-yard gap between the Japanese forces and the northern shore of Singapore.

The island was now besieged. Even then, the British leadership remained convinced that the final Japanese assault would come from the sea. Throughout all of 1941, the British commander in Singapore, General Percival, had refused to significantly strengthen the defences of the northern part of the island, as he felt that such measures would be bad for the morale of civilians and troops. As a result, my father and his fellow gunners, fortified by a daily ration of rum, continued to man a large gun battery facing southward out towards the ocean.

The generals were sadly mistaken. On 8 February, the Japanese succeeded in getting troops across the Johor Strait and securing a foothold in the north-west corner of the island. On 11 February, their engineers were able to repair the causeway, allowing tanks and mechanised vehicles to drive across. Even at this late stage, the British Commander-in-Chief for Malaya and the Dutch East Indies (now Indonesia), General Wavell, refused to acknowledge reality. His Order of the Day read, in part:

> It is certain that our troops in Singapore Island greatly outnumber any Japanese who have crossed the straits. We must destroy them. Our fighting reputation is at stake and the honour of the British Empire. The Americans have held out in the Bataan Peninsula against far heavier odds, the Russians are turning back the packed strength of the Germans, the Chinese with an almost complete lack of modern equipment have held the Japanese for four-and-a-half years. It would be disgraceful if we yield our boasted fortress of Singapore to inferior forces. There must be no thought of sparing the troops or the civilian population and no mercy must be shown to any weakness. Commanders and senior officers must lead their troops and if necessary, die with them. Every unit must fight it out to the end and in close contact with the enemy.

His words fell on deaf ears. The troops and civilian population were completely demoralised. Within a few days, they had almost completely run out of water, food, petrol and ammunition. In the end, General Percival decided that further resistance would be futile. On Sunday 15 February 1942, the so-called 'impregnable fortress' surrendered and about 100,000 Allied servicemen became POWs.

Don Kennedy, FMSVF gunner No. 13906, was among them. He had not fired a single shot.

Don's Japanese prisoner of war record, 1945

The Japanese had not anticipated having so many prisoners and initially were uncertain about what to do with them. After a few days, during which some prisoners were even able to return to their homes to collect belongings, they decided to assemble the prisoners in six compounds in and around Changi Jail in the north-east part of Singapore Island. A warning was issued that any POW found outside the Changi perimeter after 20 February without permission would be summarily executed.

Feeding so many prisoners was also an issue. The Japanese were contemptuous of those who had surrendered, as this was taboo in their military culture of *bushido*, and so initially refused to supply any food. When the British Army food reserves ran out, however, they reluctantly agreed to provide one cup of rice (often infested with weevils) three times a day for each man, as well as some drinking water. No meat, vegetables, fruit, salad or other source of nutrition were given. Soon some of the men began to show signs of vitamin deficiency and malnutrition. Others managed to cope somewhat better, at least at first. For example, some members of the FMSVF had continuing contact with local merchants, so many food and medical items were smuggled into the camps. A thriving black market developed. No one realised that these conditions would be far superior to what lay ahead.

Don spent three months in Changi. One day, a fellow prisoner approached him and informed him that there was another Irish POW named Kennedy in a distant corner of Changi – perhaps they were related? He went looking and was amazed to discover that the other Kennedy was his older brother, Fr Dick. I can only imagine the joy (and shock and concern) that both brothers experienced during this unexpected reunion, thousands of miles from home.

Dick (Richard) was a Jesuit priest, born in November 1906 and ordained in 1939. In 1941, he had answered a call for volunteers to be military chaplains for the British forces. Completely unknown to Don, he had the misfortune to be the padre on the last British Navy ship to arrive in Singapore before the surrender. He had the rank of captain (Service No. 185226) in the Royal Army Chaplain Corps. As officers typically had better access to food than regular soldiers, it seems likely that he helped Don obtain extra nutrition during the time they spent together in Changi.

Dick ultimately spent six months in Changi, later being transferred to camps in Taiwan, Fukuoka in Japan and finally Manchuria in 1945. He tried to learn Japanese but did not know about the subtle class distinctions of the language. When he tried to speak to his Japanese

Father Dick Kennedy, 1940s

guards, he spoke as a superior to an inferior. This resulted in many facial slaps and beatings.

Early in April 1942, the Japanese asked for 3,000 POWs to form a working party in the city of Singapore. Many of the men were keen to go, to escape the monotony of prison life in Changi. The British leaders decided that a large number of the Volunteer forces should be included, as they knew the city well – and so Don was among those chosen. Leaving his brother behind in the camp must have been difficult for him. He would not reunite with

Dick again for many years, though at the time he must have wondered if he'd ever see his brother again.

The day of departure from Changi came on 15 May 1942. Early in the morning, Don was among a group of 650 men – including a full company of FMSVF, which was designated as 'D' Battalion – that were ordered to march 15 miles to the Havelock Road Camp in Singapore. This was a gruelling ordeal in the tropical heat. The men had to carry 15 to 20 pounds of kit each, even though most had been existing on a semi-starvation diet for three months, further aggravated by dysentery and beriberi (deficiency of vitamin B1). Men started to collapse from sheer weakness soon after they set out on the march. The Japanese guards saw this and did allow occasional rest periods; they were not as lenient later in the war. En route, several Asian shopkeepers showed compassion to the prisoners, taking considerable risks to give them water, food and even money.

Don and the other POWs arrived in an exhausted condition at Havelock Road in the late afternoon. The camp consisted of multiple wooden huts roofed with attap palm leaves. They had originally been erected in the early part of the war, before the fall of Singapore, to house refugee Asians from the Malay peninsula. Prior to that, the whole area had been used by the local people as a refuse dump. The huts were in terrible condition, overrun with rats, bugs, lice and fleas. Neither were there any latrines. Regardless, the prisoners were too exhausted to do any tidying that evening and just slept wherever they could. One man died during the night; many more would die from Japanese ill-treatment, illness and exhaustion in the years to come.

The next day, under the direction of their medical officers, they began the general clean-up of the camp and setting up of basic sanitation, washing and cooking facilities. Conditions there soon became much better than they had been at Changi. The British soldiers were confined to the camps at night, but during the day they went out in working parties around the city. The food was not too bad and was supplemented by food bought outside or donated by friendly locals. This was particularly true for volunteers like Don, as they had the best local contacts, certainly compared to regular soldiers who had not previously lived in Singapore. Consequently, the number of sick prisoners dropped to the lowest level they would see throughout their captivity.

The work in Singapore was varied, including clearing up the city, the demolition of derelict buildings and walls, as well as building big warehouses on a piece of waste-land nicknamed 'The Cabbage Patch'. Later, when the prisoners learned that these warehouses were intended to be occupied by Japanese soldiers, they made great efforts to collect bugs, lice and fleas, leaving them there to torment their captors. It was a small act of rebellion, perhaps, but one that likely helped with morale, as Don and his fellow POWs struggled to see any quick end to their captivity.

———

At the end of May 1942, six months after the start of their offensive, the Japanese had achieved all their war objectives in Southeast Asia at minimum cost to themselves. They had complete control of Hong Kong, the Philippines, the Dutch East Indies, Thailand, Malaya, Singapore (which they renamed Syonan), all the island groups in the western Pacific, and Burma. Never before had such a large area been conquered in such a short time. They also had possession of Korea and a large portion of Chinese territory from Manchuria down to Shanghai, as well as holding every Chinese port of any significance further south. Furthermore, they occupied all of French Indochina and part of New Guinea. The Japanese called this empire 'The Great East Asia Co-Prosperity Sphere'. It extended almost 4,000 miles in each direction, occupying five different time zones – although the Japanese imposed Tokyo time throughout the captured territories.

The Allies were deeply shocked by the defeats they endured. There were fears that Australia might be the next invasion target, and these fears were compounded by an air attack on the Darwin Naval Base in February 1942, when 11 ships were sunk and the town evacuated. There was even concern that India might be overrun, or that the west coast of North America might be attacked.

The Japanese leadership, however, had a problem. They realised that their supply lines were over-extended and that Allied counter-offensives on land and sea would be difficult to resist. As the most distant of its new possessions, the defence of Burma was vital. It was extremely important that it should have ready access to troop reinforcements and war materials, which would come mainly from Thailand. In 1942, this traffic between Thailand and Burma could only happen by sea, a distance of almost 2,000 miles between Bangkok and Rangoon. Japanese merchant ships would be vulnerable to attack, by air and sea, by increasingly stronger Allied forces. But the two capitals were only 350 miles apart by land. Therefore, in June 1942, Japan made the momentous decision to link the two: it would build a railway.

The chosen route for this railway ran from Nong Pladuk in Thailand, already a stop on the Singapore-to-Bangkok railway line, to the Burma Railway at Thanbyuzayat. The new route would link these points by crossing the mountains dividing the two countries via the Three Pagodas Pass, a distance of 420km (250 miles), 310km of which was in Thailand with the remaining 110km in Burma. The greatest attraction of this route was that, for about 60 per cent of its length, it would follow the valleys of two rivers. These were the Mae Klong (or Khwae Yai – 'Big Kwai') and its tributary, the Kwai (Khwae Noi – 'Little Kwai'). This was an important factor because in Thailand in 1942 there were few roads, therefore rivers were often the main means of travel and communication. The junction of the two rivers was at the district town of Kanchanaburi. This was only 50km north of Nong Pladuk, and an existing motor road already linked the two towns. Kanchanaburi is surrounded by agriculturally productive lowlands and could act as a supply base for the railway operation on the Thai side.

Ultimately, the railway would necessitate the building of a large number of bridges (688) to cross the two main rivers and their tributaries; most of these bridges were wooden and sometimes temporary. However, at least seven were built with steel and concrete piers and

The Bridge on the River Kwai
(© Shutterstock / Wuttichok Panichiwarapun)

were intended to be permanent. Six were constructed in Burma, over tributaries of the Kwai. Only one was built in Thailand, spanning the Mae Klong, but it would eventually become world famous. Thanks to the 1957 Oscar-Winning movie, the bridge at Tamarkan near Kanchanaburi is known everywhere as 'The Bridge on the River Kwai'.

The Japanese authorities knew that the railway needed to be built quickly. Despite many challenges, they decided that it had to be completed by the end of 1943 at the latest. Of course, they needed specialised railroad equipment, including locomotives, wagons, passenger coaches and running railway line to achieve this. Most of these were requisitioned from Malaya, where a 200-mile stretch of the East Coast Railway was ripped up and 20 to 50 per cent of its inventory of diesel engines and wagons were moved north to Thailand.

Despite the already-stated benefits of the chosen route, it also contained many obstacles. The terrain was a barrier – much of it was an impenetrable, uninhabited jungle where malaria was endemic and the local rivers provided an ideal medium for the spread of cholera. Weather conditions were also incredibly difficult, ranging from intolerable heat in the later stages of the dry season (November until March) to the monsoon rains in September and October.

There was also an almost complete lack of heavy construction equipment and excavating machinery in the area. The Japanese decided that they would replace this with a commodity they had in almost limitless supply: manpower.

The 1929 Geneva Convention, which provided strict guidelines regarding the compassionate treatment of POWs, had been signed by Japan but never ratified by its parliament. The Japanese government therefore decided that they would ignore the Geneva Convention and use the POWs as forced labourers or slaves to build the railway.

———

Back in Singapore, Don and his fellow prisoners began to hear rumours that a major move north was in the offing. No other information was provided. All they knew was that parties of about 600 men would be chosen to go to Singapore station and that these men could take with them whatever they could carry.

These unfortunate men, also known as the 'Sweat Army', were made up of British, Dutch, Australian and American POWs. Their labour would be supported by many more Burmese, Malay, Tamil and Thai workers, or 'romusha', whose governments were friendly to the Japanese and so strongly encouraged them to volunteer.

On 5 June 1942, the fifth railway regiment of the Japanese Army, with some ceremony, erected the 0.0 km post at Nong Pladuk station in Thailand.

Work on the Death Railway had begun.

Japan's plan was that work would commence simultaneously at the Burmese and Thai ends of the railway, continuing until the advancing railway lines met in the middle. The first work party of 600 left Changi for Singapore city on 18 June 1942, with four more similarly sized groups following them at two-day intervals. Many others departed sporadically over the next few months.

Those left behind remained unaware of their fellow POWs' ultimate destination.

For a time, the prisoners in Havelock Road Camp had a radio receiver and were able to hear some general war news from London. However, they eventually had to dispose of it as the Japanese Secret Police – the vicious Kempeitai – were becoming suspicious. Discovery of the radio would have been punished by beheading or a firing squad – the same punishment they threatened to administer to anyone who attempted to escape, or to Asians who helped the British. This threat, as well as the general distrust of the Japanese towards to POWs, was made clear to all the prisoners in September 1942, in what became known as the Selarang Barracks incident.

On 30 August 1942, four Allied prisoners – two Australian and two English – were recaptured after attempting to escape from Changi prison. The Japanese commander, Lieutenant General Fukuye, then ordered that every POW sign a pledge, which read, 'I, the under-signed, hereby solemnly swear on my honour that I will not, under any circumstances, attempt to escape.' This directly contravened the Geneva Convention, which specifically allowed for the right of POWs to attempt to escape. They refused to sign the pledge.

The next day, the Japanese crammed about 15,000 prisoners from the Changi area (luckily, my father was in Singapore city at the time) into the parade ground of the Selarang Barracks, which measured about 128 metres by 210 metres. The troops were packed in like sardines in sweltering heat. The Japanese cut off the water supply to the toilets, so the prisoners had to dig trenches to act as latrines. There were only two taps from which to collect water. Men lined up all day to fill up a one-quart (about 0.95 litres) water bottle. This was their daily ration for drinking and washing. Still, the prisoners refused to sign.

On 2 September 1942, the senior Allied officers were taken to Changi Beach to witness the execution of the four escapees by firing squad. These men were Corporal Rodney Breavington, Private Victor Gale, Private Harold Waters and Private Eric Fletcher. The initial volley was non-fatal, which meant that the unfortunate POWs had to be finished off by further shots at close quarters.

For three more days, the POWs at Selarang held out, until the Japanese threatened to cut off water completely and move hospital patients from Singapore city to Selarang. Diseases like dysentery and diphtheria were already spreading, so Lieutenant Colonel E.B. Holmes ordered the men to sign the documents of non-escape. They did so, though many used false names. Among the

Australian prisoners, the legendary outlaw Ned Kelly was a popular choice.

The rebellion was over, if not forgotten. After the end of the war, at a trial in Singapore, Lieutenant General Fukuye was found guilty of war crimes and sentenced to death. On 27 April 1946 he was executed by firing squad at the same spot on Changi Beach where the four POWs had died. After shouting *'Banzai'*, the traditional Japanese battle cry, he died instantly.

All POWs of the Japanese, in Singapore and else-where, were forced to sign the non-escape document. There were a few other minor attempts at resistance, but the Japanese simply threatened to shoot all who refused. They were not bluffing. Everyone signed, including my father. No one felt bound to obey it.

03 THE DEATH RAILWAY

THAILAND, OCTOBER 1942

In early October 1942, the men in the Havelock Road Prison Camp were informed that they would soon be travelling north. By this time, they were generally in better health than when they had left Changi. They had stopped losing weight, and there was much less evidence of vitamin deficiencies. This was partly because the Japanese rations had improved slightly, but mostly because those in the FMSVF, including my father, remained able to smuggle food obtained from friendly local vendors into the camp.

They left Havelock Road for the last time on 12 October 1942. Their captors had ordered them to pack up their belongings that morning, long before it was actually necessary. Eventually, at about two in the afternoon, dressed in rags and carrying heavy backpacks, the group marched out of the camp to Singapore train station. Many were glad to be on the move – despite the blazing tropical sun overhead – and naively hopeful that their new base would provide better conditions.

When the exhausted prisoners arrived at the city station, they found a long train made up of enclosed steel goods wagons waiting for them. These were 18 feet long and 7 feet wide, and the guards pushed 32 prisoners and their personal possessions into each one of them. The heat and stench in the trucks was unbearable. The overcrowding was so bad that there was no room to lie down. There were no sanitary arrangements. After several hours, the guards finally allowed the sliding doors to be opened to allow some air to circulate, but the metal sides and roof remained too hot to touch.

The train made a slow crawl up the Malayan Peninsula, only stopping twice a day. The interval between stops proved too long for some of the prisoners who had dysentery; they had to perform gymnastics, leaning backwards out of the open door to relieve themselves, with friends holding their arms as the train rattled and shook its way north.

Gunner Stan Henderson gave a more detailed description:

> The procedure was to stand, legs apart and trousers down, in the doorway facing inwards; two men would hold on to each hand so that one could hang one's middle section as far outside the truck as was possible. A shout of warning was then given to the next truck and from then on matters took their own course. Before the night was through, the atmosphere in our truck was almost unbearable. Several of the men had badly soiled garments which were too valuable to throw away, but too filthy to wear, and these accumulated as the night wore on.

Thirteen hours after leaving Singapore, the train made its first stop: at Seremban, on the way to Kuala Lumpur. This provided a brief opportunity for the prisoners to toilet, albeit in open space and in full view of the local population, much to the delight of the Japanese guards. No food was provided. After 30 minutes, the train moved on, and did not stop again until it arrived at Kuala Lumpur soon after dark. Here the starving and dehydrated prisoners were given a cup of boiled rice, which they ate on the station platform. This was their first meal since leaving Singapore the previous afternoon. They had also been provided with little water and would scramble to get some at each stop, often going to extreme lengths. For example, the engine driver would sometimes let them have some from the engine. This was warm and tasted unpleasant but at least it was safe for drinking.

The prisoners still had no knowledge of their final destination, nor how much longer their ordeal in the train would continue. After an hour in Kuala Lumpur, they were moving again. This time they got more organised, as none of them had slept since they left Singapore. They piled all the personal baggage in a corner of the wagon and arranged space so that eight men could lie down at one time, feet to face, and get a few hours' rest, before being replaced by the next eight-man shift. Those waiting their turn to sleep had to sit close together in great discomfort in the limited remaining space.

The next morning, on 14 October 1942, they arrived at the town of Perai, opposite the island of Penang. Here, mercifully, the men were allowed a few hours to stretch their legs and chat with some friendly locals. They also discovered where they were going, thanks to a railway porter who came along sticking labels onto the trucks. They read 'Ban Pong'. By asking around, they learned that this town was in Thailand, and that a great deal of railway equipment had already been moved there.

The Japanese planned to build a railway going all the way to Burma, and obviously, the POWs would be the manual labourers to make this a reality. This dashed all their hope that conditions in their new surroundings would somehow be better than they had been in Singapore.

Before they left Perai, they were issued another cup of boiled rice. This was the last food issued to the prisoners until they reached Ban Pong three days later. The train continued its sluggish journey north, with only a couple of brief stops each day to break the monotony and discomfort.

Eventually, on the morning of 17 October 1942 – five days and four nights after leaving Singapore – 'D' Battalion arrived at Ban Pong. They had travelled about a thousand miles and were starving and exhausted. They were not to know it, but they had just arrived at 'The Railway of Death'.

A Japanese officer, Colonel Ishii, was at the station to greet them. He stood on a soap box and welcomed them to Thailand. He often referred to the Japanese benevolent spirit of *bushido* during this initial speech, although the prisoners – when they saw how they were to be treated – soon began to call it the spirit of Bullshitto.

Ban Pong is about 5km from Nong Pladuk, the starting point of the railway. However, since work on the railway had been ongoing for four months by this time, the headquarters for the Japanese railway engineers supervising the project had advanced to a place called Tarsau, about a hundred kilometres away. The weakened, demoralised prisoners were told that they would have to start marching there the next day. Don and his colleagues were devastated.

'D' Battalion went from the train station in Ban Pong through the small town to a nearby camp located in a paddy field. Because it was monsoon season, the ground was completely waterlogged and filthy. There was a Japanese guardhouse near the entrance and beyond it were long lines of prisoners' huts ranged close together.

The type of huts here became the standard camp building along the railway because of the abundance of bamboo and attap/palm leaf needed for their construction. The common pattern was to have bamboo walls, about three metres tall, which were about eight metres apart at the base, with attap roofs, the sides of which sloped down to half a metre from the ground. The buildings were long and quite murky, as light could only penetrate from openings at each end of the hut and in the middle – that is, apart from the little admitted under the low eaves. Within the huts, bamboo platforms extended along the length of each side. These were covered with split and flattened bamboo, which formed the communal beds. Each man had a section of these platforms just over a metre wide on which he had to sleep and store his few possessions. Down the centre of each hut ran the common passageway, which was about two metres wide. The hospital huts, at Ban Pong and elsewhere, were the same format; to get close to a patient, the medical staff often had to get onto the sleeping platform and crouch or kneel beside him.

The structure and conditions caused many problems. For example, the stagnant water which pooled below the sleeping platform was an ideal breeding ground for mosquito larvae. The attap roofs also sheltered swarms of mosquitoes, while the bed platforms provided habitats and feeding grounds for armies of insects, lice and ants. The men of 'D' Battalion were too exhausted to notice that day. Consequently, two weeks later, almost all of them – including Don – came down with malaria.

Another major health hazard was the latrine pits. These were often quite shallow and situated too close to the huts. In the rainy season, they overflowed, endangering everyone.

In these horrendous circumstances, Don and his mates had one major stroke of good fortune – their

Dr Stanley Pavillard

medical officer, Dr Stanley Pavillard, known to all as 'Pav'. He and my dad, who were the same age, had become good friends in the Havelock Road Prison Camp. He was quick-witted and resourceful and had the courage to stand up to his Japanese captors, under trying and dangerous circumstances.

He was also knowledgeable about tropical diseases, having received additional education on this topic at the University of Edinburgh, as well as practical pre-war experience in Penang and Singapore. This distinguished him from many British medical officers, the majority of whom lacked the skill and knowledge of their more experienced Dutch and Australian counterparts.

Pavillard, with only the most primitive instruments and a minimum of medical supplies, would become a hero to the prisoners on the River Kwai.

———

The next day, 18 October 1942, it was time for the prisoners to begin marching to Tarsau on the River Kwai. Before dawn, the weakened men of 'D' Battalion formed up in a column under their commanding officer, Major Clark. Some had boots, while others were barefoot. They were all, however, poorly dressed in filthy clothing and had to carry heavy backpacks containing any precious possessions they had salvaged from Singapore. In addition, Pavillard asked many of the men to carry extra parcels containing portions of medicines and supplies. This could have been the straw that broke the camel's back, but no one refused the request, meaning that all this precious cargo made it safely to their destination. They discovered later that other work parties had made the mistake of trusting the Japanese to deliver their medical supplies to the relevant camps. These were never seen again.

Trudging along on hard ground in tropical heat, the men were soon soaked in sweat. Due to this, and a lack of dietary salt, many began to experience severe abdominal and muscular cramps, forcing them to walk doubled up, which seemed to slightly relieve the pain. Others had blisters form on their heels, so they had to remove their boots and walk barefoot on the hot road. Almost all discarded some of their luggage to lighten their load.

The first agonising day's march brought them to a village and camp called Tamuang. Next day, at six in the morning, the torture began again as they walked with their heavy loads to the town of Kanchanaburi, which was about half of the total distance to Tarsau. Japanese guards used their rifle butts to hurry men along if they seemed to be struggling.

When they arrived at the larger camp in Kanchanaburi, which the POWs called 'Kamburi', the exhausted men collapsed. Pavillard and his assistant, 'Pinky' Riley, worked far into the night, treating their ailments from the march, particularly blisters. Using a rusty scissors and dissecting forceps, Pavillard punctured the bulging blisters, then cut away the loose flaps of sodden skin; Riley applied antibiotic sulfanilamide powder and adhesive dressings.

The next day was supposed to be a welcome day of rest. To the prisoners' horror, the Japanese commandant announced to Major Clark and Pavillard that the march would resume the following morning. When the British officers objected, stating that at least 250 men were incapable of walking, the commandant responded with an angry scream and slapped them both across the face. Undeterred, Pavillard told him that some of the men might die and those deaths would be the commandant's responsibility. For this insolence, he was slapped again, although immediately afterwards, the commandant agreed to give the men an extra day's rest. Sensing his advantage, Pavillard asked to be allowed to go into the nearby town with a guard to purchase medicines and dressings. Again, his request was granted.

On the following afternoon, Pavillard walked into Kanchanaburi accompanied by a guard. Earlier, he had asked the prisoners for voluntary offerings of cash, and they had responded generously; as a result, he carried a large stash of Malayan dollars with him. The chemists in town were happy to accept Malayan currency, so he was able to purchase a considerable quantity of good-quality medicines, which would later prove invaluable. As they were leaving the pharmacy, the doctor and his guard were greeted by a well-dressed Thai merchant, who invited them into a back room in his shop to drink some beer. Soon, while the guard was distracted by the beer and a pretty Thai girl, Pavillard and the merchant were able to talk in private. The merchant introduced himself as Boon

Boon Pong (© The Australian War Memorial)

Pong. This encounter was to be another significant reason for Don's survival on the River Kwai.

Although he did not reveal it immediately, Boon Pong (actually Boonpong Sirivejjabhandu) was a key member of the underground Thai resistance movement: the 'V' Organisation. In this initial meeting, he simply briefed Pavillard on the current situation in the area. For example, he explained how Tarsau – the prisoners' stated destination – was actually a staging headquarters for the railway project. The prisoners would be dispatched from there to various other locations up and down the river to clear the jungle, construct camps and prepare the ground for the laying of the track. Before departing, he asked

Pavillard for a list of the most urgently needed medicines and promised to bring these, and other wanted goods, in the course of his extensive trading by motorboat on the river. Pavillard could not believe his good fortune.

The next morning, the men of 'D' Battalion were on the march again – although without 150 men who were too sick and had to be left behind. (These men were later brought upriver by barge to rejoin their comrades.) The rest made their way along narrow jungle tracks and flooded paddy fields, struggling to bat away the incessant swarms of mosquitoes. Not that they were the only creatures feeding on them; at times they had to go through swampy marshlands and would find leeches attached to their legs. The leeches would suck blood until they were bloated, and only then could they be pulled off, leaving a smear of blood behind.

The jungle became thicker and more oppressive as they progressed. Again, the men only had rice once a day for food and boiled muddy water from the river for drinking. Drenching rains continued throughout their journey, and their kit became soaking wet and much heavier, while the ground became muddier. The men continued to develop blisters on their feet, slowing their progress, but this only resulted in them being beaten and herded onward by Japanese soldiers using heavy bamboo sticks.

It took them four days to reach Tarsau. Finally, at 10 p.m., they arrived at a large camp with the usual array of bamboo huts surrounded by huge jungle trees. The starving men were fed some rice and fell into an exhausted sleep.

They stayed in Tarsau for three days while the Japanese commanders decided where to send them. Don and the other soldiers who were fit enough were kept busy during this period building more huts. Pavillard continued to treat the legs and feet of men with blisters and cuts, which in some cases developed into large tropical ulcers – infections that had a grim reputation of worsening to the point of needing to amputate the limb. Throughout the entire war, however, Pavillard did not have to perform a single amputation on the men under his care.

Finally, the men of 'D' Battalion were told their fate. They were to travel back down the river to a place called Wang Pho – which the POWs pronounced 'Wampo'. It would be my father's home for the next six months.

04 SLAVE LABOUR

WAMPO, OCTOBER 1942–JANUARY 1943

For a pleasant change, the prisoners did not have to march to their new base, which was about 40km south of Tarsau. Instead, the Japanese guards herded the men, about 40 at a time, into barges. The barges were towed downriver by a motorboat known to the Thais as a 'pom-pom' because of the noise made by its single-cylinder engine. Once they were under way, to save fuel, the engine was stopped and they drifted silently on the strong current. On this occasion only, they were able to fully appreciate the unspoiled, untamed beauty of their jungle surroundings under a clear blue sky. Thick vegetation, sometimes interspersed with massive bamboo trees, grew right down to the water's edge. The silence would occasionally be shattered by the sounds of exotic birds and parrots or the jabbering of monkeys.

As they neared Wampo, the pom-pom's engine restarted and guided them to a mooring post by the riverbank. Once on dry land, the prisoners were put to work clearing the jungle. At this point, the Japanese had only cleared a small area, on which they had built a large hut for themselves and two smaller huts. These two huts could only accommodate a small proportion of the prisoners, so the majority initially had to sleep in the open air, with no protection from the ever-present mosquitoes.

The priority for the POWs in the first few days was to clear jungle, erect huts and dig safe, deep latrines. This was back-breaking work. The manual labour of the prisoners was aided only by some rope, hammers, axes and dull two-handled saws. In addition to the thick tangle of smaller vegetation, there were numerous clumps of tenacious giant bamboo and large hardwood trees. These trees were often secured to their near neighbours by intertwined branches and a mass of creepers – sometimes two or three would have to be sawn before one could be felled. Meanwhile, the bamboo stumps had to be pulled out of the earth one stalk at a time, each stalk needing up to 10 men pulling on a rope to unearth it.

After two weeks of arduous work, from 8 a.m. to 6 p.m. every day, the accommodation was much better. By this time, 11 huts, one hospital hut, cookhouses, stores, latrines and drains had been completed. Don's 'D' Battalion had also been joined by two other battalions, 'B' and 'F', during this time, bringing the total number of prisoners to just over 1,500 men. The British commanding officer was Lieutenant Colonel H.H. Lilly. The Japanese commandant was Lieutenant Hattori Hiroshi, while the senior Japanese non-commissioned officer (NCO) was Sergeant Takeda.

One thing which did not improve was the food supplied by the Japanese. The quantity was inadequate, particularly considering the manual labour the men were doing, while the quality was terrible. Since there was no rail or road access, food supplies had to be brought into the camp via the river. The river could be too fast-flowing during the wet months and not deep enough in the dry months, so deliveries were not reliable, with 8- to 12-day intervals between food deliveries on barges being common. Rice and vegetables were practically the only source of nutrition for the men. No meat or oil was issued by the Japanese until 20 December 1942, while sugar and salt supplies were infrequent.

When deliveries did arrive, the polished white rice was often dirty and in large bags weighing 220lb, which

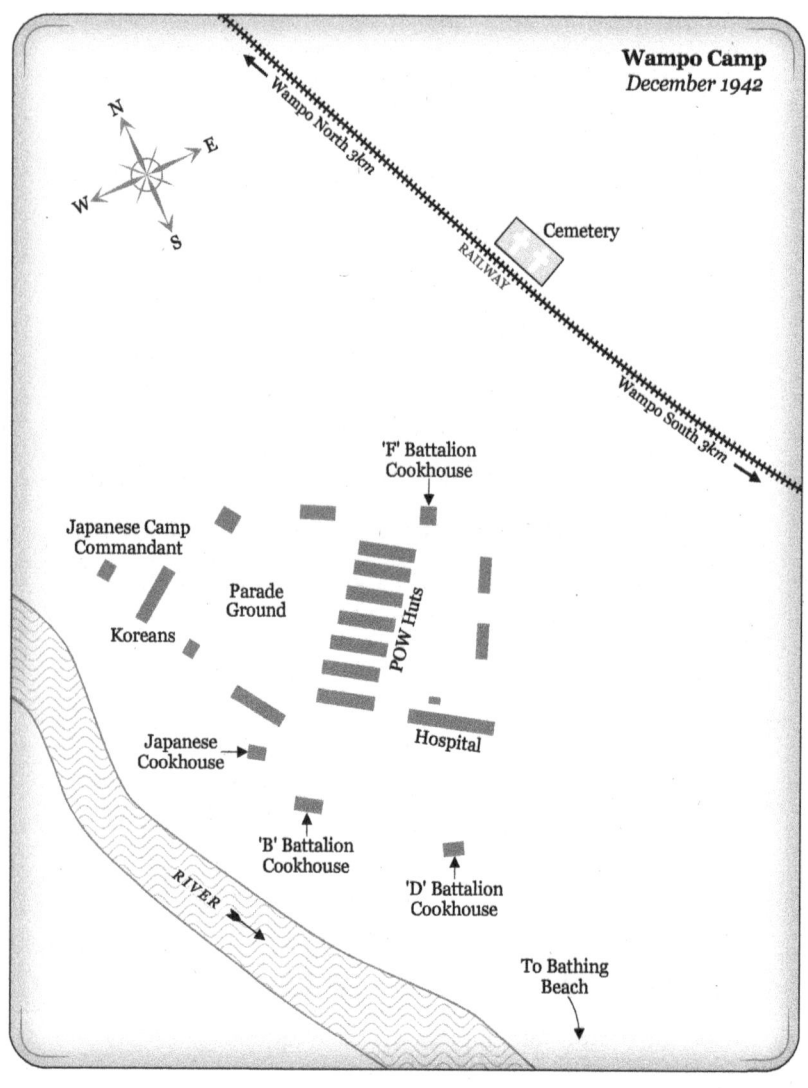

Wampo Camp
December 1942

N
E
W
S

Wampo North 3km

RAILWAY

Cemetery

Wampo South 3km

'F' Battalion
Cookhouse

Japanese Camp
Commandant

Parade
Ground

POW Huts

Koreans

Japanese
Cookhouse

Hospital

'B' Battalion
Cookhouse

'D' Battalion
Cookhouse

RIVER

To Bathing
Beach

had to be carried by the men from the river up a steep bank to the store houses. Vegetables – commonly marrow, cucumber, chinese radish or sweet potato – were partly rotten on arrival and frequently too rotten to use after about four days. Soon, because of the growing malnutrition and semi-starvation, the cooks served up the rotten vegetables anyway.

The Japanese basic rations per person were as follows: rice – 750 grams; tea – 5 grams; vegetables – 500 grams; salt – 5 grams; sugar – 3 grams; oil – 4 grams; meat – 3 grams. As I previously mentioned, sugar, oil and meat were rarely available in the first two months at Wampo. As a result, a typical day's menu consisted of a breakfast of boiled rice and tea with a level dessertspoon of sugar if available, and dinner (at midday) of boiled rice, tea and salt. The evening meal was rice, thin, watery vegetable stew and tea.

Not surprisingly, in view of this, the number of sick men in camp began to increase rapidly. Because of salt deficiency and inadequate calories, many suffered from low blood pressure and had distressing blackouts if they raised their heads too quickly. Most had blistered feet or small ulcers, while a few showed early evidence of vitamin deficiency. Diarrhoea, acute and chronic, was common. Because of all the mosquito bites on their march to Tarsau, malaria became widespread. The Japanese refused to give

Dr Pavillard enough quinine for treatment, only allowing a small ration for each man. To counteract this, he classified all the sick in the camp as having malaria, thereby gaining a greater supply of quinine for those who genuinely had the illness. Because of this, and the supplies he had bought earlier in Kanchanaburi, the men at Wampo received much better malaria treatment than those at other camps.

————

The work of building the railway line began in earnest in mid-November. The Wampo section of the line was to be about 12 miles long and would entail an embankment for a single railway track, along with a viaduct at the south end and a bridge at the north end. The initial work consisted of clearing a path ten metres wide through virgin jungle, mostly by hand. These paths were known as cuttings. The laying of track would come later.

Within those cuttings, the commonest task for the POWs at this stage was the construction of embankments. These were raised earthworks, which were necessary to maintain a gentle gradient along the railway. They ranged from slight elevations in places, simply to level out uneven terrain, to massive artificial hills in other parts. For example, one embankment was seven metres tall.

The embankments were built from rock and soil. Sometimes this material would be available close at hand from the excavation of cuttings, but often the necessary materials had to be dug up further afield by a group of POWs and romusha. The diggers used basic tools such as shovels, picks and hoes (also called chunkels). These tools were of poor quality and they regularly broke. When the material was dug up, it would be delivered to the embankment site by other POWs using baskets or a sack spread between two bamboo poles, known as a 'tanka'. Once it was delivered, the men had to stamp down the earth at the top of the embankment and return to the diggers for more.

The daily quota for each man was to move one cubic metre of earth. Even though they became progressively weaker and more exhausted, their Japanese taskmasters gradually increased this quota. Work for the prisoners began at 8 a.m. and finished at 6 p.m., with a one-hour dinner break at midday. For the first few months, they were given a rest day every 10 days.

The Japanese also informed the men that they would be paid for their work. However, sick men would not be paid, they explained, and their food rations would be cut in half. Ordinary ranks such as my father were paid 20 cents a day; NCOs (corporals and above) 25 cents a day; warrant officers 30 cents a day, and officers 30–50 dollars a month (scaled according to rank). Ultimately, most of this money went into a canteen fund, which was used (when possible) to buy extra food for the sick, as well as cigarettes and tobacco for the working men.

Later in November 1942, walking through the jungle, Dr Pavillard met a Thai farmer looking after some cows. Dr Pavillard tried his luck at striking a bargain with the farmer for a cow. His most useful currency was medication and so, after some haggling, the farmer agreed to sell one of his cows in return for a bottle of 250 quinine tablets. The transaction was completed the next day and some Australian POWs put their butchering experience to good use. That evening, every one of the prisoners consumed half a pint of somewhat watery but delicious meat stew.

After this delightful episode, the British commanding officers approached the Japanese commandant, Lieutenant Hattori, with a proposal: they would purchase cattle from the Thai farmer every few days using cash from a meat fund to which all the prisoners would contribute. They were pleasantly surprised when he said that he had no objection to the idea and actually welcomed it. He admitted that there was no likelihood of meat being supplied by the Japanese high command until the railway line reached the camp, which might take several more months.

My dad and his fellow prisoners were fortunate that Hattori was in charge at Wampo. Unlike many other Japanese commanders of POW camps, he was well educated and spoke perfect English. Furthermore, he was not a career soldier – in fact, he had been a lawyer before the war and had taught at the University of Tokyo. Most important, he seemed sympathetic to the plight of the prisoners, understanding that many of them could die without better nutrition.

To everyone's relief, the meat purchase scheme worked well. Every third day, the prisoners were able to buy a skinny cow or water buffalo. Although the Japanese guards helped themselves to some of the meat, there was still enough left over to give the men more protein in their diet. Consequently, their morale improved a little.

Unfortunately, soon after, the Wampo prisoners had their first death. A young soldier, Lance-Corporal Hutchinson, died of severe dehydration caused by acute dysentery with associated vomiting and diarrhoea. At this relatively early stage of construction, the Japanese guards seemed embarrassed by this and supplied planks to allow for Hutchinson's burial with a formal funeral in a small cemetery area not far from the camp. They even allowed a coffin to be made. This behaviour did not last. Subsequently, with so many prisoners' deaths, all other corpses were buried naked or in rags, with little or no ceremony.

Pavillard wrote a report to Hattori about the death, stating that Hutchinson's life could have been easily saved if he had received an intravenous saline solution, which was available in Kanchanaburi. A few days later, he was called to Hattori's hut and told to repeat his comments by an angry visiting Japanese superior officer. Pavillard stood face to face with the officer and spoke out, saying that many more men would die without a better diet and medical supplies. The Japanese would have to take full responsibility, he asserted. This type of 'disrespect' would usually have earned a prisoner a beating. For a full minute, the officer stared at Pavillard while Hattori shifted uneasily in the background. Then the unexpected happened – the officer declared that Pavillard and Hattori would be allowed to travel to Kanchanaburi to get more supplies.

I suspect that the Japanese officer recognised Pavillard's courage in his readiness to fight for the welfare of the men under his care and that this earned his respect. Hattori may also have persuaded him that preventing further POW deaths was in everyone's best interests.

This news was greeted with surprise, excitement and joy by the prisoners. Soon Pavillard was inundated with money and private orders for 'luxuries' such as soap, tobacco and toothpaste.

A couple of days later, in the early morning, Hattori, Pavillard and a Japanese guard left Wampo. They sailed south, downriver, in a pom-pom. Even though the River Kwai was still running fast, they did not reach Kanchanaburi until 4 p.m. that day.

The three men proceeded to the camp where they were able to eat and find a sleeping place for the night. That evening, Hattori allowed Pavillard and the guard to go into the town. In addition to purchasing medical supplies and personal items, Pavillard tried to meet up again with Boon Pong. Luckily, he was at home. He and his family made Pavillard welcome while also arranging for the guard to have some female company elsewhere, thereby allowing the two men to speak freely.

While enjoying some local beer, Boon Pong still did not reveal his full involvement with the 'V' resistance movement, but he did tell Pavillard that, through intermediaries, he had regular contact with the Swiss Consul in Bangkok. He said the consul was willing to buy medicines for the prisoners, as well as supply additional local currency, which Boon Pong would deliver to Pavillard on his trading trips upriver. Pavillard conveyed his gratitude for this, while also informing Boon Pong about the cruel conditions in the camps. Later, they made arrangements for the next morning, when Boon Pong would supply Pavillard with a variety of drugs and also 100kg of peanuts and rice polishings, which would be full of the vitamins the prisoners needed.

This was delivered in a handcart the next day, as planned, and loaded into the trio's pom-pom. As they returned to Wampo, Pavillard would have undoubtedly thought of the trip as a major success.

———

Despite the tough labour and working conditions, and the inadequate diet, the mood in the camp remained good. Lieutenant Hattori continued to cooperate, even allowing the prisoners to hold a camp concert. This featured a number of 'chorus girls' dressed in costumes made from odd bits of cloth and tree bark, with wigs made from old rope, and makeup from ground flour and some tree sap. The show was attended by many of the Japanese guards, who kept going behind the scenes to ensure the beautiful ladies on show were in fact prisoners and male.

By December 1942, however, the work demands at Wampo were becoming ever harder. During the day, there was intense heat and humidity in the jungle conditions, followed by cool evenings. The malnourished men felt this cold intensely and had to build big fires to keep warm. Every day, the engineers set a target of a certain amount of jungle to be cleared and embankment to be built; the working party was not allowed to return to camp until the work was completed. If a man in the party became sick, he was not replaced, but the same amount of work still had to be done. Loss of fluid from sweating put men at risk of collapse from dehydration and heat exhaustion. To avoid this, the guards would allow two of the least healthy men in a work party to make a fire and brew watery tea.

Pavillard noted how more and more of the men were suffering with dysentery, malaria and vitamin deficiency. The men on his sick list were excused from work. Every day, over and above the actually ill patients, he would allow an extra 15 men to 'go sick', making it possible for each man in rotation to get an extra day's rest.

On 20 December 1942, the British Quartermaster at Wampo received an allocation of meat from the Japanese for the first time – a 10-stone pig. However, this was expected to last two days and feed over 1,500 men, even before the Japanese guards took one-fifth of it for themselves. By this point the starving prisoners had become much less fastidious about what they ate; they would catch and kill a snake, an iguana or even a monkey to supplement their protein intake. They had also learned how some creeper that grew abundantly around the camp could be boiled up and eaten to increase the vegetable supply.

On Christmas Day 1942, three pigs were issued to the prisoners. The menu on that memorable day was as follows: breakfast – rice with two spoons of sugar, tea and two pieces of peanut toffee; dinner – pork stew, extra vegetables and peas, pork dumplings and rice tea; tea – pork stew, vegetables, rice, pork dumplings, two eggs and tea. Every man was also given an extra 20 cigarettes each.

I imagine that Don slept contentedly that night. At that time, he had little to no knowledge about the progress of the war. He certainly would not have known that the tide had started to turn against the Japanese months earlier. In June 1942, in the most important naval battle of the entire war, they had been defeated in the Battle of Midway by a smaller American fleet. American forces had also landed on Guadalcanal in the Solomon Islands in August 1942, and the Japanese forces there would soon surrender. Likewise, Australian and American forces were overwhelming the Japanese army in Buna, New Guinea. The Japanese empire was shrinking.

Similarly, Don and his mates knew little about the overall progress of the railway. He certainly had no inkling that in 1943 it would truly become 'The Railway of Death'.

———

In January 1943, the work routine in Wampo was much the same as it had been in the previous two months. By this time, due to the extremes of jungle weather, most of the men found that their army-issue shorts and shirts had rotted away. They resorted to wearing what was known as a 'Jap-Happy': a simple loincloth consisting of a long piece of white linen approximately six inches wide with two pieces of string attached to the ends. The string was tied around a prisoner's waist while the rest of the material was drawn forward from behind under the groin to cover the genitalia. The loose end just flapped down in front. This attire was not dignified but was comfortable and functional. While the man's skin was now exposed to the burning tropical sun, and mosquitoes, he was less likely to be bothered by lice and bed bugs under his clothing.

Each morning, the prisoners were woken by guards shouting 'All men worko' and rattling canes across the bamboo walls of each hut. After a brief latrine visit, they formed a line for the usual rice breakfast. The POW cooks would already have been up for a couple of hours, heating two 12-gallon cast-iron saucer-shaped pots of rice (known as 'kualies') and boiling drinking water in cauldrons over an open fire.

After breakfast, the men were paraded outside the huts for 'tenko', i.e. the roll-call. This was overseen by a Japanese drill sergeant, a 'gunso', and enforced by Japanese or Korean guards. The count, or 'bango', was conducted in Japanese. If a prisoner made a mistake calling out his number, he would be beaten – sometimes having a rifle smashed into his face – and the count would begin again. Men could also be beaten if they did not stand to attention, bow or salute at the approach of a guard. Sometimes several beatings would occur, meaning the whole process could take up to an hour.

After the count was complete, the prisoners lined up for tools. Sharper tools such as saws and chisels, which the Japanese feared might be used as weapons, were always kept at the worksite. After collecting their tools, the men marched to the site. The only men left behind at camp were the designated sick, the medical officers and their assistants, the few officers and the cooks.

On one memorable day in early 1943, Dr Pavillard was called away from his medical duties and marched to the guard room by the Japanese. There, much to his surprise, was Boon Pong. He had arrived via the river and had aroused suspicion when he asked for Captain Pavillard by name. Fortunately, this was forgotten when he announced that he had 10,000 duck eggs for sale and gave each guard a dozen eggs for free. After this giveaway, it was agreed with the British commanding officers that the remaining eggs would be purchased for five cents each. That day, Don Kennedy and all the other members of 'D' Battalion must have stuffed themselves with eggs. More than a few likely suffered a restless night after their orgy of food, I suspect.

Boon Pong had also brought supplies of medicines that Pavillard had requested at their previous meeting. No payment was necessary for these as they had been paid for by a special fund started by the Swiss consul in Bangkok, Herr Walter Siegenthaler, and another Swiss national, Herr Tanner. This was only a half-truth. We will learn more about the source of these funds in a future chapter. One thing is certain; these drugs, and the previously supplied rice polishings, saved many lives.

Through all this, Don's thoughts must have turned often to home. To Nora.

05 DEAD OR ALIVE?

IRELAND, 1943

Back in Ireland, one year after the surrender of Singapore, my mother was frantic with worry. She had no idea whether her fiancé was dead or alive. And even if he was alive, she had no knowledge of where he was being detained.

This was because, as previously stated, the Japanese government refused to honour the terms of the 1929 Geneva Convention regarding the humane treatment of prisoners of war. Japan had sent three representatives to that convention, who signed the agreement along with representatives from 46 other countries. However, it was never formally ratified by the Japanese government. Still, in February 1942, they stated that, while they were not bound by the convention, they would 'respect its terms – in respect of English, Canadian, Australian, New Zealand and Indian prisoners of war'. It is clear, however, that they did not.

The Geneva Convention had a total of 97 provisions. For my mother and other next of kin of the Japanese POWs, the most important provision involved the role of the International Committee of the Red Cross (ICRC). Under the convention, the ICRC was expected to act as a central agency for the exchange of information between the warring nations concerning their respective captives. There was excellent compliance in this regard in Europe. By mid-1942, relatives of POWs in German and Italian camps were even receiving a monthly magazine, *The Prisoner of War*, featuring extracts from prisoners' letters home, news regarding Red Cross parcels received and sometimes photographs of POW football teams and hobby groups.

In stark contrast, by the end of 1942 there was still no information from the Japanese about their Malayan prisoners. Finally, in January 1943, relatives of 1,100 men who had surrendered in Singapore received cards indicating that they had been captured. No other information was provided. Don Kennedy's relatives were not included.

By this time, Nora had returned to Mallow to live with her mother. She hadn't been able to complete her degree programme in UCD, as, in her third year in college, she had developed a chest infection and a chest X-ray showed possible scarring of her lungs. A pulmonary specialist recommended abandoning her studies to reduce her stress levels. Once home, she never returned to university.

She did, however, frequently visit Don's parents in Dublin. She was warmly welcomed at Hollywood, their conversations often involving speculation about the well-being of Don and his brother Dick. Don's mother remained hopeful that they were alive, but his father was convinced that they were dead. No doubt this was not what Nora wanted to hear.

She regularly enquired for news about her fiancé from the Colonial Office in London. In early April, she received a response from that office dated 31 March 1943. The letter read as follows:

In reply to your letter of the 20th March I am directed by the Secretary of State for the Colonies to say that he regrets that no further information has yet been received in this Office regarding your fiancé, Mr F.W. Kennedy [sic]. Telegrams are,

however, now being received at the War Office
from Tokio [sic], through the International Red
Cross, giving the names of military prisoners of
war captured in Malaya and now interned in
Malayan camps. The telegrams so far received
include the names of some members of the local
Volunteer Forces and a few civilians, and the next
of kin in these cases are being notified as quickly
as possible. The name of Mr. F.W. Kennedy [sic]
has not appeared in any of these telegrams, but
no significance need be attached to this omission
since only a small proportion of the names of
the British subjects in Japanese hands in Malaya
have so far been received. The Secretary of State
deeply sympathises with you in your anxiety, and
desires me to assure you that any information
regarding your fiancé that may be received in this
department will be conveyed to you with the least
possible delay.

More heartbreak.

For the next couple of months, it was difficult to
keep up her usual positive attitude. Her friends and sister
were supportive, insisting, for example, that she go with
them to dances on Saturday nights at the local tennis

club, which she thoroughly enjoyed. Not surprisingly, she had her share of admirers. If they became too interested, however, she simply asked them to admire her engagement ring.

To keep busy, she would sometimes help her mother in the drapery shop. One day in May 1943, she was asked to open a packing case of new clothes. The packing in those days usually consisted of old newspapers. On this occasion, there were also several small prayer cards devoted to St Anthony. She wondered if this was a sign, and began praying to him.

Within a couple of weeks, she received a letter confirming that Don had been interned in a Malayan camp.

Tears of joy flowed down her face. She believed that the good news was thanks to St Anthony, initiating a devotion to him that she retained for the rest of her long life.

Communications on this subject
should be addressed to—

THE UNDER SECRETARY OF STATE,

COLONIAL OFFICE,

~~LONDON, S.W.1.~~

and the following 206/16079/1/43
Number quoted :

Your Reference

~~Downing Street.~~

Enquiries and Casualties
Department,
2, Park Street, W.1.

4 JUN 1943

Madam,

I am directed by the Secretary of State for the Colonies to
inform you that telegrams are being received from Tokio, through the
International Red Cross, giving the names of military prisoners-of-war
who were captured in the Far East and are now interned in Malayan camps.
Among the names received are those of some members of the local Volunteer
Forces, and the following entry appears in one of the telegrams:—

"KENNEDY. F. D. 13906 . Interned MALAYAN CAMP"

As this list of names emanates from the Japanese authorities
in Tokio, the information contained in this letter may be regarded as
official.

2.   In all cases where it is known that relatives or other
enquirers are resident in a Dominion or Colony, the information is
being conveyed by telegram to the appropriate authorities for
communication to the persons concerned.

3.   Full information regarding the sending of letters to
prisoners-of-war in Japanese-occupied territories in the Far East may
be obtained from any principal Post Office.   It is regretted that, at
the moment, no facilities exist for sending parcels or remittances to
prisoners and internees in Malaya.

I am, Madam,
Your obedient Servant,

S. J. Cole

Miss Nora Ring.

The second letter received by Nora,

confirming Don's whereabouts

06 SPEEDO-WORKO

WAMPO, JANUARY-MAY 1943

> 'The Japanese are prepared to work – you must work. The Japanese are prepared to eat less – you must eat less. The Japanese are prepared to die – you must be prepared to die.'
>
> Lieutenant Usuki, Commandant, Konyo No. 2 Camp

In the early months of 1943, it became ever more clear to the Japanese leadership that the tide of the Pacific War was turning against them. On the island of Guadalcanal, after a long and bitter campaign, their troops were withdrawn at the end of January, leaving behind nearly 15,000 dead. Similarly, organised resistance in Papua was almost over, with a loss of 12,000 imperial soldiers. Most naval battles by now resulted in victories for the American Navy. Likewise, the Japanese were consistently losing naval ships (34 in January 1943 alone) to attacks from US submarines and the British Eastern Fleet. Unlike the Americans, the Japanese did not have the manufacturing capacity to replace these lost ships with new vessels. As a result, the Japanese could not spare any battleships to act as an escort for their merchant navy travelling around the Malay Peninsula and up to Rangoon, which meant that these ships were increasingly vulnerable to attack.

Because of this, one of the Japanese River Kwai Railway engineers was summoned to Tokyo in January 1943 to provide an update on their progress. To his amazement, he was told that the railway now had to be completed by the end of May 1943. When he pointed out that this was impossible, it was reluctantly agreed to move back the completion date by three months, meaning the railway would have to be operational by the end of August 1943. Thus began the horrors of the 'Speedo' campaign.

My dad and his mates at Wampo were, of course, quite unaware of the reasons for 'Speedo'. However, they quickly noticed the dramatic changes in their work routines that made life harsher for everyone. For example, rest days or half-days were eliminated. The camps also now came under the direct command of the Japanese railway engineers. The engineer in charge at Wampo was Lieutenant Ibuka, who was much less tolerant than Lieutenant Hattori. He insisted that more men should go out to work on the railway. Despite the pleas of Dr Pavillard, many of the less sick men were sent to work, while cookhouse and administrative staff were reduced.

To shouts of 'Speedo-Worko', the men set off to work before dawn and returned late at night. The quota for moving earth was raised to three cubic metres a day per man. Guards were instructed to beat the men if they did not work harder to hit these quotas – and they did so frequently.

In addition to the lack of clothing, boots were becoming a thing of the past for many prisoners – they were falling apart and could not be repaired. So the POWs had to work barefoot, or with a piece of wood underfoot, held in place by a piece of cloth.

Due to this relentless new routine, they had no time to wash themselves or air their bedding, so the number of lice and bugs increased. Skin diseases, especially scabies and ringworm, attacked everyone, while cases of malaria, dysentery and beriberi became much more common. Still, the sick men were expected to work; if they were excused, their rations were reduced.

The engineering work at Wampo was regarded by the Japanese as one of the most challenging parts of the railway construction. Unlike other areas where the riverbank was sandy and flat, here it was rocky and cliff-like. The engineers decided to carve out a narrow ledge halfway up the cliff face as a base for the railbed. Then, to carry the railway, they (or rather, their slave labour) would construct an immense wooden viaduct about a half-mile long through the long S-bend that the river and rock made at this point. This area became known as Wampo South.

Likewise, about 3km north of the Wampo camp, the engineers needed another shorter length of rock ledge, about 150 feet above the river – this was named Wampo North. Two subsidiary camps were built at these locations.

———

At the beginning of March 1943, Don and the other men of 'D' battalion were moved to Wampo South. At the same time, another 2,000 POWs, most from other camps and some new arrivals from Singapore, arrived at Wampo. Many of these men had to sleep in the open, as no further accommodation was available. At Wampo South, the subsidiary camp was located on some flat ground near the river, on the opposite side from the high cliff where the railway was being built.

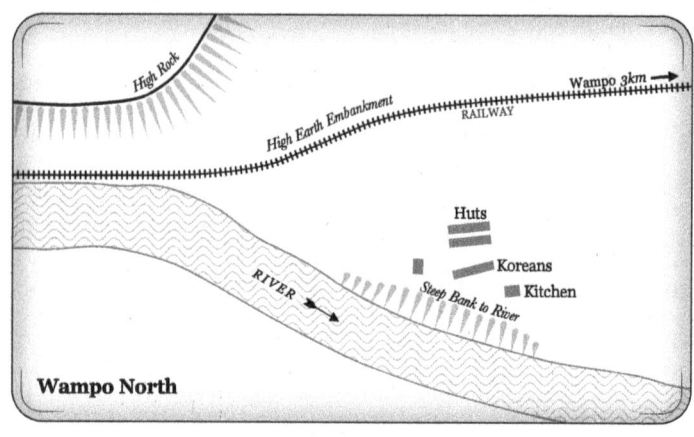

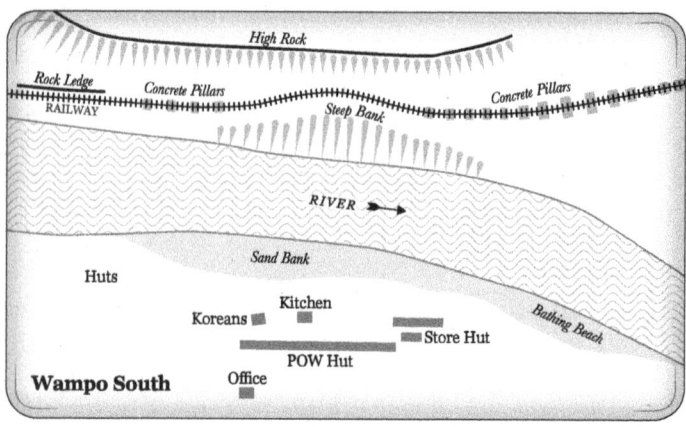

The prisoners working on the cliff face had to cross the River Khwae Noi to go to the railway construction site each morning. Initially, this was not too difficult, as it was the dry season and so the river was quite shallow. Once across the river, the work on the cliff face was strenuous and quite dangerous. On a ridge high above the ground, the men were completely exposed to the blazing sun and heat. The scorching rock hurt their feet. The glare of sunlight from the bare rocks burned their eyes. Some collapsed from heat exhaustion.

Hundreds of tons of rock had to be removed from the rock face. This was done using explosives provided by the Japanese and the manual labour of the prisoners. The process went like this. First they drilled a deep hole using a 'chisel', which was actually a long thin piece of metal. One or more prisoners held the chisel against the rock while their workmates hit the other end with a hammer until they had made a hole deep enough to accommodate a charge of dynamite. The metal was not always solid; sometimes chips and splinters could fly off, causing open wounds that could easily turn septic in the hot, dirty and dusty conditions. For the same reason, the tip of the chisel could also become embedded in the hole. The labourers would then have to team together to try to pull it out by hand. If any of them lost their footing, or were too weak or exhausted, they could easily slip off the ridge, falling from a considerable height onto previously dislodged rocks or into the river. This was often fatal but was seen to be greeted with laughter by some of the guards.

When several holes had been prepared in the rock, dynamite would be dropped into each one. It was then expected that a warning signal would be given, whereupon the men would take cover and the fuses were lit, usually using a cigarette, by the Japanese guards. Sometimes, however, the guards would not bother to give a warning, just for the 'fun' of seeing the prisoners scrambling for shelter. When the British officers complained about this behaviour, they were told it was the men's own fault and that they should get out of the way more quickly.

On one occasion, the prisoners did manage to get a small amount of revenge. This was when a section of cliff face opposite the Wampo South camp was being blasted. Unknown to the Japanese, the job of drilling the holes was allocated to some experienced gunners. Perhaps Don was involved. These men had received extensive training in firing large-calibre coastal guns and were expert in calculating trajectory and distance in order to hit a target. On the day when all the holes were ready, the charges were laid and the fuses lit by Japanese soldiers. A loud bang and large shower of dust followed. Across the river, large rocks and assorted debris fell on the camp, which was unusually empty of prisoners. The projectiles landed mainly around the Japanese hut emplacement, causing quite a bit of damage. This was greeted by loud cheers from the prisoners. Of course, they professed total innocence in the aftermath – after all, the Japanese had placed the dynamite and lit the fuses. This episode became known as 'The Gunners' Revenge'.

While the ordinary prisoners continued their work at Wampo South – where Don was – and Wampo North, Dr Pavillard and the other medical officers remained behind at the old Wampo camp, travelling back and forth to visit patients. On 10 April 1943, Pavillard was at the camp when, looking down a jungle path, he was surprised to see a new group of British POWs approaching. They were escorted by Japanese guards and were carrying a total of 18 heavy packages slung on long bamboo poles. He recognised that these packages were British field medical panniers – specially designed wicker baskets used to transport medical supplies. He briefly became excited that the Japanese were going to provide medicines for the Wampo prisoners. However, his hopes were soon dashed. The work party unloaded their precious cargo at the camp rice store, far from the hospital, and it was placed under lock and key.

Pavillard was full of curiosity about the mysterious cargo and got talking to one of the British soldiers in the work party. He learned that the panniers contained British drugs captured when Singapore fell. It turned out that they were only to be left at Wampo overnight, as the work party would continue its journey the next morning. Ultimately, the drugs were to be used for the benefit of Japanese soldiers further north.

He could not resist the temptation to find out what medicines were in the panniers. As previously described, the 10-feet walls of each hut did not reach the roof. Without notifying any of his fellow doctors or officers, he got Pinky Riley to act as a lookout and scrambled over a wall and into the rice store. The panniers were only tied with wire and string. The first one he opened was full of tins, each tin containing 1,000 'M & B 693' tablets. These were the first generation of sulfonamide antibiotics and were precious, as they were effective against numerous bacterial infections, including trop-ical diseases. (Later that year, this medication was given to Winston Churchill to successfully cure pneumonia.) He placed a tin inside his tattered old shorts, tied up the pannier and departed. He and Riley then buried the tin.

Later that day, Pavillard discussed the situation with his fellow medical officer, Captain 'Daddy' Richardson. They both knew that this was a golden opportunity to improve the medical care of their patients. The Wampo stretch of railway line was nearly completed, so it was likely that they would soon be moving up country again. Furthermore, Boon Pong had not brought supplies for quite some time, and it would be harder for him to do so if they ended up even further north from Kanchanaburi.

They went to the officers' hut to meet with Lieutenant Colonel Lilly, the British camp commandant, as well as Majors Clark and Brodie, the commanding officers of 'D' and 'F' Battalions respectively. Pavillard and Richardson requested permission to plan another raid on the medical supplies before they left Wampo. After a prolonged discussion, Colonel Lilly decided that this was too dangerous. Their reasoning was that the Japanese commandant lived close to the rice store and there might be extra guards on duty later on. There was also the reality that, if they were caught, any men participating in the raid would be decapitated.

Pavillard was devastated. He foresaw how, without extra supplies, medical care further upriver would be significantly worse than the current conditions. The more he thought about this, the more determined he became. He would defy his commandant's orders.

By this time, some of the prisoners had returned to camp from their work on the railway. Pavillard spoke to four men from the FMSVF about his idea and their part in it, should they agree to help. He also reminded them that, if captured, they would suffer torture and execution. Their names were Lance-Corporal E.T. Miles, Sergeant T.P. Cassidy, Private K.T. Wadsworth and Quartermaster J.M. Metcalfe. They all volunteered without hesitation.

Everyone was sworn to secrecy as the plan was worked out in detail. In the dark, the panniers could not be properly examined in the rice store. Therefore, the plan was that, once inside the rice store, two men would lift each pannier over the partition, while the other two would carry it 25 metres to a medical examination room attached to the hospital. There, Richardson, Riley and Pavillard would examine the contents with a light and remove a reasonable quantity of needed medications. The pannier's remaining contents would then be rearranged to disguise the theft and returned to the rice store. As this went on, Riley would take the stolen drugs and bury them.

The operation began at 9 p.m. A few other trustworthy men were brought along to act as sentries, without being fully informed as to what was going on. They were to give a prearranged whistle if any Japanese appeared.

For the first entry, Pavillard accompanied the two men to show them exactly where the panniers were in the rice store. The coast seemingly clear, the trio began to climb the bamboo partition. At that moment, they heard the danger-signal whistle. Panicked, they dropped down the far side of the partition and crouched in the darkest corners they could find inside the store.

Their hearts pounded as they heard the footsteps of a Japanese guard marching towards them. Time seemed to stand still.

After an eternity of suspense, they heard the guard's footsteps recede. Soon after, an all-clear whistle sounded. Now the work could begin.

Pavillard helped the men lift the first pannier over the partition and to the hospital as the other two men entered the store, looking to prepare the next pannier.

They rapidly developed an efficient rhythm. As soon as they finished extracting a few life-saving drugs from one pannier, another would arrive. There were no further alarms.

Smooth progress continued until the second last pannier. As Pavillard reached in, he felt a sharp pain in the middle finger of his right hand. He struggled to suppress a scream of agony, sure that he had been bitten by a snake, which could be fatal. To his relief, further inspection revealed a scorpion. The sting would be painful for a week but not life-threatening.

Finally, the last pannier was returned to the store; the operation was over. It was 2 a.m. Pavillard thanked his four volunteers, complimenting them on their speed at lifting the heavy panniers over the 10-foot partition. Embarrassed, they confessed that they had not exactly followed instructions. Instead, they had opened the door of the rice store from the inside and brought the panniers out that way. Hearing this, Pavillard almost passed out. The door of the store was opposite the hut of the Japanese commandant.

Next morning, to everyone's relief, the Japanese guards and the prisoners carrying the panniers moved out of the camp without incident. There was no suspicion of foul play. As soon as they were gone, Pavillard confessed his insubordination to Lieutenant Colonel Lilly. Lilly replied, 'I had a notion you would do it, Pav; as a matter of fact, I haven't slept a bloody wink all night.'

The treasured medications were left buried for several days in case there was any delayed discovery of the theft. There was none. Once dug up, they were divided equally between the medical officers for 'D', 'B' and 'F' Battalions in preparation for their move upriver. The bravery of the participants in this adventure was to save countless lives in the months to come.

———

Meanwhile, at Wampo South, the slave labour continued for Don and his fellow prisoners. In fact, it intensified. Having completed the blasting to create a rocky ledge, now the wooden surface of the viaduct had to be completed.

On the west side of the river, where the POW camp was located, many of the men were now directed to stay behind. The camp was situated on the edge of a forest of teak trees, which would be the source of timber for the trestles for the viaduct. They were felled by the POWs using only handheld saws, which was exhausting work as the wood was extremely hard. Japanese engineers then cut it to the right length and squared it up using an adze.

The completed, heavy, squared beams then had to be moved down to the riverbank. Of course, no machinery was available. However, the Japanese on this occasion did provide some assistance to the prisoners – namely, a few elephants, with their Burmese trainers, or mahouts. These remarkably intelligent animals were able to lift and carry the beams before depositing them at the river's edge with precision and apparent ease.

But there were not enough of them. So, once again, the starving, malnourished prisoners had to do much of the heavy lifting. Depending on their length, the beams sometimes weighed up to three-quarters of a ton. Initially, the men tried to carry them like an undertakers' team with a coffin on their exposed shoulders, but the edges of the wood were rough and sharp. Instead, eight or ten stout bamboo poles were pushed under the beam and, with one or two men holding each end of the poles, the huge pieces of teak could be carried down to the river.

The first time the Japanese engineers tried to float a giant beam across the river, they discovered to their cost that the green teak was too dense. It sank. From then on, the beams were fastened to bundles of bamboo to keep them afloat and the prisoners swam them across.

Meanwhile, on the east (cliff) side of the river, the other team of prisoners removed all the boulders created by the blasting. Next, concrete foundation piers for the trestles had to be built. For these, the Japanese engineers set up wooden shutters, while the POWs – using rice sack stretchers – carried heavy, wet hand-mixed concrete to the site.

Once the piers were in place, the trestles had to be erected. Since there were no cranes, intricate bamboo scaffolding was fastened to the cliffs above the rocky ledge and pulley blocks were fastened to the scaffolding. A long thick rope was then run over the pulleys, and a team of about 50 prisoners would raise each beam into its proper position – first the vertical beams and then the even heavier horizontal cross beams. Metal spikes were used to fasten the beams together. One prisoner, Captain Barry Baker, estimated that between 500 and 1,000 beams were used to build the viaduct. As each trestle and section of the structure was completed, other groups of POWs got busy laying down sleepers and rails on top of it.

The work was reminiscent of biblical times. Two shifts, each of 1,000 men, worked from before dawn until 2 a.m. the next day. All the while, to push on an exhausted workforce, beatings by the guards increased, using bamboo, iron bars, spades, rifles or any other object close at hand.

At the end of April, the monsoon rains began. This made conditions even more dangerous for the men working on the viaduct. The Japanese did not care. 'Speedo' continued mercilessly.

Finally, on 10 May 1943, the railway line reached Wampo North. That day, Don and his fellow prisoners stood and watched as the first train engine emerged from the mist and rattled by in a cloud of steam. Perhaps they thought that this might have justified some celebrations or well-deserved rest. There were none forthcoming. Instead, they were instructed to prepare to move up country.

Each battalion would have a different destination. For my dad's 'D' Battalion, the destination was Tonchan South.

Somehow, his nightmare was about to get even worse.

07 CHOLERA

TONCHAN SOUTH, MAY–AUGUST 1943

By this time, after 15 months as a POW, Don was sick and exhausted. Like all his colleagues, he suffered from malaria, which caused terrible drenching night sweats. These continued for a time even after the war ended. He was fortunate that, thanks to Dr Pavillard and Boon Pong, there was an adequate supply of quinine tablets, which were taken daily to reduce or sometimes eliminate the symptoms. Unfortunately, unknown to Pavillard, some of the men refused to take quinine because of side-effects, which could include severe tinnitus (ringing in the ears), hearing loss, flushing and headache, confusion, disturbed vision, nausea and abdominal pain. Occasionally, for some of these men, the disease would progress to severe cerebral malaria, whereby they would present with a fever of 105–107 degrees Fahrenheit (40–41 degrees Celsius) and complete debilitation. Once the condition was recognised, treatment consisted of aggressive cooling of the entire body and administration of intravenous quinine (made by dissolving quinine tablets in a home-made saline solution, which was injected into a vein). The man would be placed completely naked on the ground, fanned and doused continually with cold water. Without immediate treatment, their temperature would rise to 110 degrees Fahrenheit and the unfortunate prisoner would become delirious and sink into a coma. After this, there was no hope of recovery, as the brain was literally fried. After they died, the pills they were supposed to have taken would be found hidden under their rice-sack pillows. Those who were fortunate enough to survive usually had no memory of what had happened. Otherwise, they made a full recovery.

There was no way to avoid malaria. The men had almost no clothing and certainly no mosquito nets. They worked in a thick jungle full of mosquitoes and were always on the move. The railway construction was their only priority, so there was never time to use oil to destroy the mosquitoes' breeding grounds.

Don was also severely underweight and malnourished. Still, at this stage, he was much more fortunate than others. Due to the terrible monotonous diet, diseases caused by vitamin deficiencies, such as beriberi and pellagra (vitamin B3), were becoming common. Infectious diseases other than malaria were also widespread. These included bacillary (bacterial) and amoebic dysentery, diphtheria, typhus and tropical leg ulcers, as well as ringworm and scabies.

Even at this stage (and conditions were to deteriorate further), up to 60 to 120 men per month were dying in many of the POW camps. By contrast, Dr Pavillard reported in the *British Medical Journal* of 26 January 1946 that at Wampo, after seven months, they had lost only 15 men, and that three of these deaths had been due to drowning. This was undoubtedly thanks to the excellent medical care provided by Pavillard, as well as the extra medical supplies obtained through theft and the efforts of Boon Pong.

Nevertheless, all the men based in Wampo were sick and starving. Still, the Japanese deemed that few were sick enough to be excused from railway construction. On 17 May 1943, 150 very sick men were moved by barge downriver to Chungkai POW base hospital camp. The remaining 'fit' men were ordered to go up the river to ever more isolated camps. There, they would face the worst infectious killer of all: cholera.

———

Don and the men of 'D' Battalion were the last workers to leave Wampo on 13 May 1943. As before, they had to endure a forced march northward, in torrential rain, of about 25km (15km to Tarsau and a further 10km to Tonchan South). Once again, each man was laden down, carrying kit, cooking utensils and a portion of the medical supplies. At first, the march followed the railway tracks and the ground which had been levelled in preparation for them. Further north, however, they had to cross crude wooden bridges spanning some deep ravines. These had been built in a clumsy fashion using jungle tree trunks and felt unsafe to walk over. This was because the POWs doing the construction had taken every chance for sabotage, leaving spikes and bolts loose or in the wrong place. Still, they were forced across. Eventually, when the Japanese sent heavy goods trains over these bridges, many collapsed, in some instances causing the locomotive to explode at the bottom of the ravine.

After walking for 20 hours, the exhausted, emaciated prisoners arrived at Tonchan South. This was a scene of unbelievable filth, mud and overcrowding. The camp already held about 3,000 POWs, while a neighbouring camp for Asian 'coolies' – mostly Tamil and Chinese workers – held about the same number of people, including women and small children. The two camps together occupied an area of less than half a square mile. It was situated on a hill above the river, but at the point of a hollow below high mountains (see map). As a result, when the monsoon rain fell, the water collected there and the ground turned to feet-deep mud. A small stream flowed through the centre of both camps, with the Allied camp downstream from the Asian camp.

The conditions for the native 'volunteer' workers were far worse than any POW camp. These unfortunate individuals had no leaders of any sort, nor did they have doctors or medicines. No record was kept of their names or origins, and they were only fed sporadically by the Japanese. Most significantly, they had no knowledge of the proper sanitation practices for their circumstances. Since they were upstream, Pavillard gave strict instructions that the men of 'D' Battalion must always boil water from the stream before drinking it or using it to clean their teeth.

Accommodation for the prisoners consisted of leaky huts or tents. When the torrential rains occurred, they

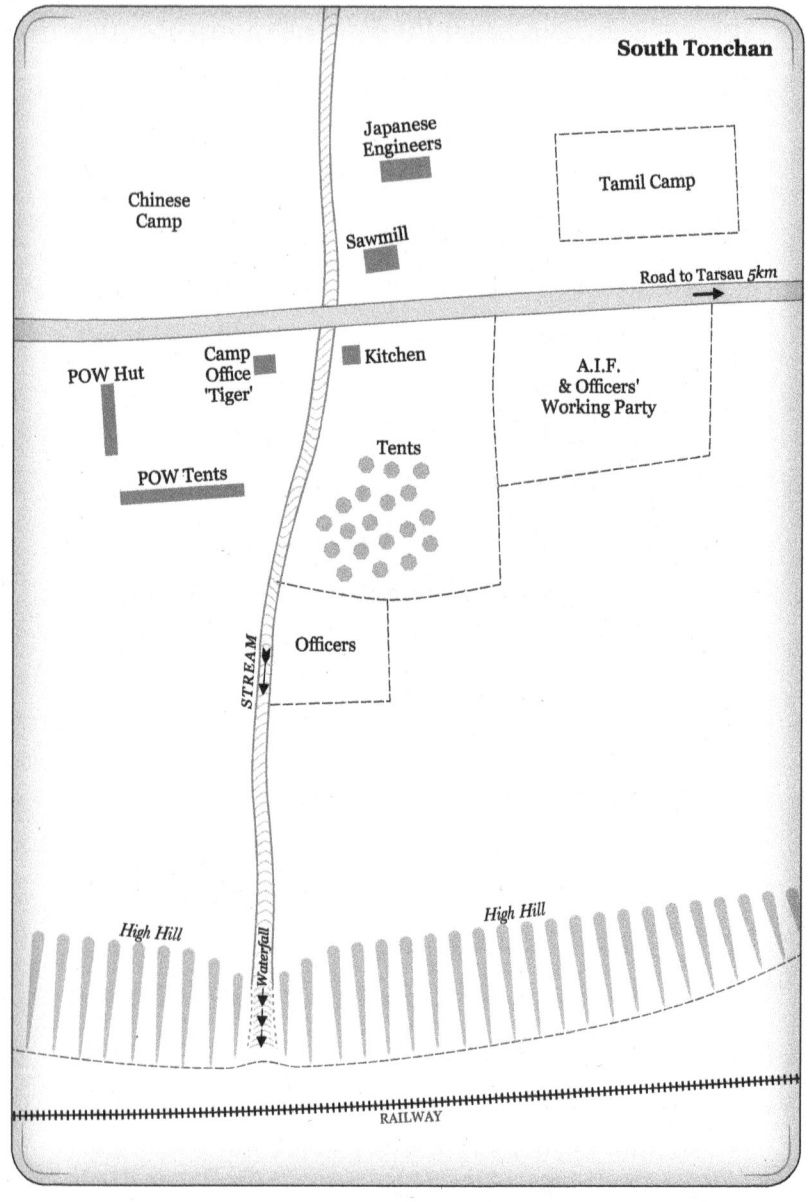

South Tonchan

Japanese
Engineers

Tamil Camp

Chinese
Camp

Sawmill

Road to Tarsau *5km*

POW Hut

Camp
Office
'Tiger'

Kitchen

A.I.F.
& Officers'
Working Party

POW Tents

Tents

STREAM

Officers

High Hill

High Hill

Waterfall

RAILWAY

were almost as wet inside as outside. The latrine situation was arguably even worse. There were only three latrines for their use throughout the camp. These were holes about eight feet long, two feet wide and four feet deep, with bamboo spanning the gap. This allowed three men to squat and use each latrine at the same time. Since there was no toilet paper, leaves or dried grass were used instead. Given that there were thousands of men, and many suffered with chronic diarrhoea, this latrine accommodation was woefully insufficient. Sometimes men would be unable to wait and were forced to do their business anywhere they could find in the camp. This made for an ideal breeding ground for flies, of course, which meant there were millions in the air. The camp, especially the cookhouse, was black with them. The men said that if you used a fly swat, you could kill 200 flies with each swat. All of this made for a perfect recipe for the spread of gastrointestinal disease, including cholera.

The Japanese commandant at Tonchan South was Staff Sergeant Hiramatsu, known as the Tiger. He was a man of few words, and was rough, tough and brutal. He imposed a ruthless discipline, both for the Japanese guards and the prisoners. On one occasion, 'F' Force, one of the last British and Australian POW parties to leave Singapore, stopped at Tonchan for a short time before moving on to camps further up the line. These prisoners, many of whom were sick when they left Singapore, had endured the five-day train journey described previously, and had then been forced to march for up to 17 days to their final destination. A British quartermaster, 'Pop' Vardy, and three others were caught trying to pass a little food and water to these unfortunate men. As punishment, the Tiger made these four men stand to attention while he paraded up and down, beating them across their backs and legs with a thick bamboo rod, which was at least two inches across. When this rod split and splintered beyond use, he picked up a metal bar and continued the beating until he grew tired. The four men were forced to stand to attention without hats for another three hours before he dismissed them so that they could receive medical treatment.

Everyone was afraid of the Tiger. So when Dr Pavillard and the camp interpreter were called to his office the day after the arrival of 'D' Battalion, he was understandably nervous. The interpreter warned him that Hiramatsu understood a lot of English but refused to speak the language of the enemy. Once before him, the Tiger asked Pavillard why so many of his men were sick; he alleged that it was because they were lazy, sleeping on the wet ground without shirts to protect them from mosquito bites. Pavillard bravely responded that the number of sick men was caused by the poor diet, overwork, inadequate accommodation and terrible sanitation. As proof of this, he explained how even though he was a doctor, and had taken proper precautions, he had still caught malaria.

He expected a beating for his insolence. Instead, after a pause, the Tiger joked that Pavillard must have caught the disease by taking girls into the jungle at night. He laughed hysterically at his own perceived wit. Pavillard decided to go along with the laughter and, to his surprise, the Tiger then agreed to improve the prisoners' food and give them half a day's rest each week.

Three days later, the Tiger sent for Pavillard again. He was shivering, obviously in the midst of a malarial attack. He demanded an injection of intravenous quinine. Pavillard turned and said to the interpreter: 'Ask him if he has been taking a girl into the jungle?' Before he could respond, the Tiger roared 'Hurrah!' at the top of his voice and reached for a sword by his bedside. However, he managed to control himself and even smiled, asking the doctor to be less comical and get on with the injection. Pavillard did so and the Tiger was up and about the next day.

———

In early June, rumours reached Tonchan that cholera had broken out in camps upriver. For the British medical officers, this was ominous news. Even for healthy individuals, cholera is one of the most serious gastro-intestinal infections. For many emaciated, malnourished POWs, it would likely be the final straw.

Cholera has been recorded historically for at least 2,500 years. There have been seven worldwide pandemics in the last 200 years, which have killed millions of people. In 1854, during a cholera outbreak in Soho, London, Dr John Snow curtailed the epidemic by removing the handle of a public water pump that he correctly believed was spreading contaminated drinking water. In addition to saving lives, this dramatic step helped to prove that it was a water-borne disease. Previously, the medical and scientific community were convinced that it was an airborne disease. This realisation led to fundamental changes in the water and waste systems in London, and later in most large cities around the world, resulting in a dramatic improvement in public health.

By sheer coincidence, and quite independently of Snow's work, the organism responsible for cholera was identified in Florence during an outbreak there in 1854.

The discoverer, Dr Filippo Pacini, named the bacterium, *Vibrio cholerae*. By the end of the nineteenth century, a safe and effective injectable vaccine was available. Because of this vaccination – but especially because of advanced water treatment, hygiene and sanitation – cholera outbreaks became rare or non-existent in developed nations early in the twentieth century. However, this was not the case in poor countries – and certainly not in the POW camps.

Conditions on the River Kwai in May–June 1943 were perfect for a cholera outbreak. It was the rainy season, and the river often overflowed its banks. All the prisoners were starving and weak. The time-bomb was ticking.

Pavillard knew the symptoms to watch out for among the POWs. In severe cases, symptoms can begin within hours of exposure. The classic symptom is the abrupt onset of large amounts of watery diarrhoea, frequently described as 'rice water' in appearance and sometimes with a fishy odour. Vomiting and muscle cramps may also occur. Within another few hours, severe dehydration and electrolyte imbalance can result. This manifests in sunken eyes, dry mouth, cold clammy skin, decreased skin elasticity and a wrinkling of the hands and feet. Without adequate fluid replacement, the patient's condition rapidly deteriorates, causing generalised weakness, impaired consciousness, laboured breathing and death. Cholera is sometimes nicknamed the 'Blue Death' because the dehydration can turn a patient's skin bluish-grey.

Pavillard did not wait for an explosion of that ticking time-bomb. He felt fortunate that about 70 per cent of his men in 'D' Battalion were well educated: lawyers, businessmen and chartered accountants like Don. He gave them lectures about the dangers of cholera and the rigorous precautions needed to prevent contracting the disease. He insisted that they should only use boiled water for drinking or cleaning teeth. No bathing in the river was allowed. Eating utensils were to be dipped in boiling water before use. Food touched by flies should be discarded. Men should try to avoid putting their hands in their mouths. He even insisted that the dirty scraps of paper they used to make cigarettes should not be licked.

Before leaving Wampo, Pavillard had asked the Japanese for some anti-cholera vaccine and been refused. However, on 7 June, he was allowed to walk to the Tarsau camp and, after renewed protestations, succeeded in getting some supplies. This was promptly administered to 'D' Battalion as soon as he returned. It proved not a moment too soon.

The next morning, 8 June 1943, a prisoner from 'F' Battalion presented with all the classic symptoms and signs of severe cholera. The medical officer of 'F' Battalion, Dr Vincent Bennett, and Pavillard, went to report the bad news to Tiger Hiramatsu. He was angry with the doctors and ordered them to move the man to the base hospital camp at Tarsau. They of course refused, pointing out that moving him would inevitably spread the disease. At this, Tiger went red in the face and, brandishing his sword, screamed: 'It is an order of the Imperial Japanese Army that the man be moved to Tarsau!'

Fortunately for the men of Tarsau, three more cases were diagnosed within an hour and so the movement of the infected man was cancelled. Tiger was by now frightened and sent for the Japanese medical officer to come from Tarsau. When he arrived, he agreed with the British doctors' diagnosis.

Despite torrential rain, they had a working party make a clearing in the jungle about a quarter of a mile from the camp, where they pitched a leaky tent provided by the Japanese. The sick men were taken there on improvised stretchers, made with a rice sack slung on two bamboo poles. By nightfall, 10 cases were packed inside the small tent, and the first man had died. Medical orderlies tried to give water to the patients, which they often vomited up, all while the doctors gave injections of morphine to ease the horrible muscle cramps.

Within two days of the original diagnosis, there were 200 cases among the prisoners. As the Japanese refused to provide any more tents to accommodate them, many of the unaffected POWs gave up their own sleeping tents so that the patients would have some protection from the heavy rain and tropical sun. With these, a cholera compound was developed next to the first tent.

To make matters even worse, cholera spread even more rapidly in the neighbouring Asian camp. Again, the Japanese refused to make any provision for them to be supplied with clean water or food; the sick were just dumped on the open ground next to the cholera compound. Untold hundreds of them died in a horrible fashion. Other infected Asians panicked, fleeing into the jungle. Since the only escape routes were via the river or its tributaries, this ensured that every available source of water became contaminated. For weeks afterwards, working parties of POWs discovered the bodies of these individuals in the jungle.

For the British POWs, the medical officers realised that the key to an individual's survival was the rapid replacement of the body fluids lost by diarrhoea and vomiting. Necessity is the mother of invention, as the old saying goes. Within a couple of days, Pavillard and his colleagues had manufactured a crude water distillation plant. This apparatus was made up of an army-type metal food container, rubber tubing (sometimes from old stethoscopes), giant bamboo and jam jars. Salt was added to the distilled water in an attempt to make a saline solution equivalent to the human body's own saline; this was administered intravenously, using a small, hollow bamboo needle. This procedure was reserved for the worst cases; amazingly, this regime worked well and saved many lives.

The medical staff also asked the Japanese for soap or lysol to clean the contaminated hands and feet of the doctors and medical orderlies, but again the request was refused. Instead, they did the best they could using wood-ash and hot water. Likewise, the Japanese would not allow British caregivers to stay in the cholera compound overnight, ordering them to return to their regular camp each evening, even though this obviously heightened the risk of increasing the number of deaths, as well as spreading the disease.

Despite the horrors of cholera, work on the railway construction never stopped. The on-schedule completion of the railway remained the only priority to the Japanese, 'even if every man died', as the Tiger put it. This meant that the Tiger refused to release fit men for the gruesome job of burying or cremating the increasing number of dead. Instead, this task was allocated to 'semi-sick' prisoners, men judged not fit enough to work on the railway but not sick enough to be bed-bound.

One of these was Don Kennedy. My dad had recently been diagnosed by Dr Pavillard as having beriberi, a condition caused by deficiency of thiamine or vitamin B1. Thiamine is found in a wide variety of foods – lentils, beans, peas, asparagus, whole grains, brown rice, pork, fish and nuts – so, given his diet, it was hardly a surprise that he finally developed the disease. The word beriberi comes from a Sinhalese word meaning 'extreme weakness'. The condition became common in Asia in the late nineteenth/early twentieth century when the European colonisers decided that polished or white rice, with the thiamine-rich husks removed, tasted better than brown or rough rice. Soon after, the disease became widespread among poor Asians, whose diet consisted almost entirely of rice. Many died. The condition was also discovered to be worsened by high levels of physical exercise.

Thiamine is essential for the effective functioning of the nervous system and muscles, as well as the heart and cardiovascular system. When a deficiency occurs, the symptoms are divided into 'dry' beriberi (which affects the neurological system only) and 'wet' beriberi (affecting the heart and circulation). On the River Kwai, both types of beriberi tended to occur simultaneously in the same individual.

Don, like many members of 'D' Battalion, was in some ways fortunate in that he had up to that point endured sixteen months of captivity, and eight months on the Death Railway, without contracting beriberi or other vitamin deficiency diseases. This was due in large part to the resourcefulness of Pavillard and Boon Pong in obtaining supplementary food such as rice husks and peanuts in addition to the monotonous white rice diet. However, his luck had now run out at Tonchan South.

When Don was examined by Dr Pavillard, he had the usual symptoms of early dry beriberi. These included weakness in his legs, some difficulty walking, tingling and numbness in his hands and feet, and stabbing pains in his feet. The tingling and pain in the feet were worse at night, and, with typical dry humour, were called 'happy feet' by the POWs. He was also emaciated by this point, having probably lost 50–60 pounds in weight.

Despite all this, he was still considered fit enough to be selected as a member of a burial party designated to dispose of the dead cholera victims. Men were dying so rapidly by this point that the Tiger ordered the digging of a communal grave. This was done by Don and his co-workers, who had to resort to using jungle vines to hoist workers and earth out of the pit as they worked. In the end, the pit measured 20 feet long, 10 feet wide and 20 feet deep.

In the first seven days of the cholera outbreak, 189 of the British prisoners died, along with a much higher number from the Asian camp. My father later recalled burying 21 of his comrades on a single day. He often had nightmares in the post-war period, and it is likely that this experience was largely responsible for them.

The conditions he worked in were horrific. The nauseating stench from the burial pit spread throughout the camp. The pit contained not only the dead prisoners and Asian labourers, but millions of flies and maggots. Each evening, the burial party would shovel a thin layer of earth over the swollen bodies. Sometimes, cremation of the bodies was attempted, which only succeeded in adding a smell of burning flesh to the other foul camp odours.

Advanced cholera can sometimes give patients a corpse-like appearance. For this reason, the British doctors would wait an hour or two after a death before the expired man was brought to the pit – just in case the patient had not in fact died. The Japanese had no such qualms. Twice a day, a Japanese orderly would inspect the area where the Asian victims lay. Dressed like a surgeon in a white coat, gum boots, rubber gloves and a mask, some may have thought him a helpful figure. However, he had not come to help. Instead, he would order the burial team to remove those he suspected were dead, even if some had not yet passed away. No mercy was shown.

————

The cholera epidemic petered out over the next few weeks, although the disease did not completely disappear. Tiger Hiramatsu was upset that there were not enough fit men working and became convinced that he could find malingerers among the sick. It therefore became his habit to parade the sick in all kinds of weather at any time of the day or night. Skeletal men, with no boots or clothing, were made to stand in black, slimy mud for an hour or more. Exhausted, they would try to hold each other up, as they were guaranteed a terrible beating by the guards if they fell.

Hiramatsu's mistreatment of sick POWs like Don was not forgotten. After the war, he was arrested and brought to trial as a war criminal in Singapore in August 1946 because of his actions at Tonchan South. One affidavit from a prisoner, R.W. Long, stated that the Tiger was: 'very cruel to the sick, driving them to work and trying to get those in hospital out by threats and beatings. He was responsible, although not personally killing any POW, for most of the deaths in the camp. Men just gave up and died, through malnutrition and over-work.'

On 22 August 1946, Hiramatsu was found guilty and sentenced to death. He and two others were hanged at Changi prison on 22 November 1946.

At the end of June 1943, the railway had reached and passed Tonchan South. The prisoners were again told to prepare for another move upriver. The Japanese authorities decreed that 550 men would move to a notorious camp called Konyu. This soon earned the nickname of Hellfire Pass. The members of 'D' Battalion were the healthiest of the POWs at Tonchan, so they provided 450 of the detachment destined for Hellfire Pass. Don was not one of them, however, as he was too weak and ill.

On 1 July 1943, Don said goodbye to his 'D' Battalion comrades, many of whom – like Pavillard – had become close friends during the dreadful experiences and suffering of the previous 17 months. They left Tonchan via the riverbank in relative luxury, heading north in barges pulled by pom-poms. Many would never return.

The remaining sick men at Tonchan South were regarded with contempt by the Japanese. As they were no longer working on the railway, their already meagre rations were cut in half. Those who were not completely bed-bound were still expected to do camp work, which included sanitation, cooking and carrying rations.

This persisted for about a month. It seems probable that the Japanese delayed the evacuation of these men to a base hospital downriver in the hope that more of them would either recover or die.

Finally, they made a decision. The 'lighter sick' were ordered to march to the nearby Tonchan Main Camp. Meanwhile, the 'seriously sick' were moved by barge to Tarsau base hospital camp. Don, now suffering from advanced beriberi, was one of these men. His outlook was grim.

08 MIRACLE

TARSAU BASE HOSPITAL CAMP, AUGUST–SEPTEMBER 1943

'Since July of this year Tarsau hospital has grown from a camp hospital into a base hospital for the whole of No. 4 Thailand group. It is through no fault of our own that it is one of the most scantily equipped hospitals in the world.'

Lieutenant Colonel Edward E. ('Weary') Dunlop, 1 December 1943

Don arrived at Tarsau hospital camp on 3 August 1943. It was one of the first three 'hospital' camps established at the southern end of the railway by the Japanese; the other two were at Kanchanaburi and Chungkai. These camps were supposedly in better condition than the jungle camps to the north, although this is debatable. The accommodation was much the same, as was the level of overcrowding.

Tarsau was probably the worst of the three hospital camps. As previously described, it had been established as a staging camp for the Allied POWs and Japanese soldiers in October 1942. By the time Don arrived, it was a large, cleared area located next to the River Khwae Noi, surrounded by big trees and roads that carried Japanese troops and supplies to Burma. These roads, running parallel to the river and the railway, were little more than tracks, with numerous potholes, stumps and rocks. They also turned into a sea of mud after heavy rain. During a monsoon they became impassable.

When my dad arrived at Tarsau, the camp consisted of 84 poorly constructed huts, many of which were near collapse; in fact, some eventually did collapse on top of their inhabitants. Each hut had the usual slatted beds teeming with bugs and lice, with about 60–80 men crowded together. Initially, there were between two and three thousand men in the camp, primarily British, Australian and Dutch. Many times that number were ultimately admitted, as work on the railway grew ever more arduous and a steady stream of sick men arrived.

Twenty-four of these huts, essentially no different from the others, were designated as hospital huts. These were separated from the rest (see map on page 164), but unfortunately located close to the river, leaving them prone to flooding during periods of heavy rain. Furthermore, there were virtually no medical supplies at the hospital, and the food was poor and insufficient. Also, there were few medical orderlies to care for the sickest patients, meaning less sick patients had to care for themselves and their hut-mates.

Morale at that time was very low. Those in charge of the hospital did not seem to have the drive or ability to lift the spirits of the men. (How Don must have missed Dr Pavillard at this point.) Every one of the patients was suffering physically, but also psychologically, from the abuse of the 'Speedo' period.

In theory, the hospital was supposed to be subdivided into separate huts for different types of patients – surgical wards, tropical ulcer wards, acute dysentery wards, vitamin-deficiency wards, malaria, amoebic dysentery, etc. There were also supposed to be some convalescent huts. In reality, little effort was made to accurately diagnose the men, and many were suffering from multiple problems at the same time.

The only real distinctions were that critically ill patients were placed in one hut, a grim place where dozens died each day, while those with infected tropical leg ulcers were also placed separately. The stench from these huts was nauseating and spread throughout the camp. These pitiful men had horribly painful, purulent and often large open wounds extending from the knee down (and occasionally above). The only conservative treatment the doctors and orderlies could offer was to scrape away the pus using a spoon. No anaesthesia was available. Following this torturous procedure, the cleaned wound would be dressed with pieces of old blankets, which had been sterilised in boiling water in nearby

Inmates of Tarsau hospital camp, 1943

44-gallon drums placed over fires. Mosquito nets were also sometimes used. If there was no improvement, the affected leg would have to be amputated. These operations, using chloroform as a general anaesthetic, were performed daily. Many of the already debilitated men did not survive the surgery.

Don was admitted to a 'medical' hut, mainly occupied by those suffering from vitamin deficiencies. By this time, he had advanced beriberi and severe malnutrition. His symptoms by this stage were a combination of 'dry' (neurological) and 'wet' (cardiac) beriberi. Wet beriberi, essentially an indication of weakness of his heart musculature, caused swelling of his legs. This carried the additional risk that if the fragile, numb skin in his lower limbs developed even the smallest cut, he could develop an ulcer. Fortunately, this never happened.

As previously described, the huts had slatted bamboo shelves running the full length of the interior on each side to serve as bedding. Don was allocated a width of about a metre of this as his own living space, with perhaps a blanket and a rice sack to place on top of the bamboo. This was sufficient for warmth, as the weather at that time of year was never cold.

The overworked doctors and medical orderlies rarely visited his hut, as they were too busy elsewhere, and in any case they had no medication with which to treat the patients. The sick men learned to fend for themselves and their neighbours. Those who were able assisted in washing and feeding the very weak.

The food in Tarsau was not much better than it had been in the camps upriver. While there were adequate supplies of white rice, vegetables were always in short supply. Meat was rarely seen, although once or twice a week the prisoners would receive a small ration of smoked or salted fish. The fitter men were still working and receiving meagre wages from the Japanese, as did the officers. Some of these funds were pooled together and used to purchase additional food for the sick from local traders. Eggs were eagerly sought after for their nutritional value, but there were never enough to go round. Sadly, for those with beriberi, they would have needed five or six eggs each day to provide them with enough thiamine for their needs – an unimaginable feat.

Over the next six weeks, Don's condition stabilised but did not improve. He remained weak and lethargic, while his swollen legs meant he had great difficulty walking even short distances. He recognised, however, that some of his fellow patients were in worse shape. In addition to their physical ailments, many suffered with depression, hopelessness and anxiety. The days and nights were long and dreary, with little to keep them occupied. Some, suffering with multiple diseases, and exhausted beyond the limits of human endurance, simply gave up. They would lose interest in people and things around them, refusing to eat or drink. Death would soon follow.

Don was determined to live. He dreamed of returning to Ireland and being reunited with Nora. It was now four years since that magical, carefree summer in Ballybunion. He had just celebrated his thirtieth birthday. His calm, stoic personality, his strength of character and religious faith helped him believe that he would survive.

To keep up morale, he and others in his hut came up with a plan to pass the time. Each man was asked to entertain the others for 5 to 10 minutes. He could do this in any way he wished – by telling a joke, singing a song, talking about a hobby or passion, reciting a poem, and so on. This became part of their daily routine and proved a welcome boost for most of the men. For Don, it would save his life.

One day in mid-September 1943, Don and his fellow patients were passing time as I've described above. When it came to his turn, he decided to speak about a topic close to his heart: Ballybunion. He described the natural beauty of the area, and why it was so important in his life. Despite the weakness in his body, his voice was clear and strong.

When he finished speaking, he was surprised to notice the arrival of an unknown white man at the main entrance to the hut, accompanied by a Japanese guard. The man was unusually well-dressed compared to the dishevelled prisoners. Don was even more surprised when the stranger walked down the aisle towards him, while the guard remained at the entrance.

The newcomer stopped at the end of Don's bed, and quietly asked him if he was the person who had been speaking about Ballybunion. When Don confirmed this, he explained that he was an Irish doctor who had been invited by the International Committee of the Red Cross (ICRC) to do a camp inspection. He had been passing Don's medical unit when he heard an Irish accent, and the mention of Ballybunion, which he knew well. My dad told him how he was an Irish citizen and had been a British civil servant in Singapore when it fell to the Japanese. He told the Irish doctor that he was now gravely ill with beriberi, and the camp doctors had no medication to treat him.

The two men conversed for a short time longer. Just before he left, the doctor warmly shook Don's hand. Fortunately, the Japanese guard did not see how, during the handshake, the doctor transferred an envelope containing some pills into my dad's palm.

For Don, these were an unbelievable treasure: thiamine, or vitamin B1, tablets. In a few moments, his prospects of survival had dramatically improved.

A chance encounter – and the utterance of 'Ballybunion' – had likely meant the difference between life and death for my father. It was truly a miracle on the River Kwai.

09 THE RED CROSS AND THE 'V' ORGANISATION

THAILAND, 1942-5

This was quite likely the first time that the Japanese authorities had allowed an ICRC inspection of a River Kwai hospital camp. While the Japanese did not feel bound by the rules of the 1929 Geneva Convention regarding the treatment of POWs, their diplomats and generals had repeatedly claimed that they would adhere to the spirit of the agreement. In fact, they claimed that POWs would be treated just as well as Japanese soldiers. This was, of course, totally untrue. Allied prisoners were starved and abused throughout Asia, and the worst mistreatment of all was on the Death Railway.

Not surprisingly, the Japanese tried to suppress any news of this from reaching the outside world and so, for most of the war, they opposed camp inspections by any neutral representatives, stating that Red Cross aid parcels were unnecessary since the prisoners were well cared for.

These were formidable obstacles to overcome. Ultimately, however, news of the horrific conditions in the River Kwai camps did reach London in 1943. Soon after, the Japanese relented and ICRC camp inspections occurred sporadically between 1943 and 1945. A few Red Cross aid parcels also started to reach the prisoners in the late stages of the war. The credit for this belongs to two organisations and four remarkable individuals.

The organisations, both based in Bangkok, were the aforementioned underground 'V' organisation and the Swiss Consulate. Two of the responsible individuals have also previously been mentioned in this book: the legendary Thai trader Boonpong Sirivejjabhandu, and the determined Swiss consul, Walter Siegenthaler. The other two were English businessmen Ken Gairdner and Peter Heath, who were among about two hundred British civilians interned by the Thai authorities in a camp in Bangkok in January 1942.

This camp was located on the grounds of a Bangkok university, where the civilian internees were relatively well treated. As a result, Gairdner was able to keep in close contact with his Thai wife, Millie, and a Chinese employee of his, K.S. Hong. In late 1942, they began to report disturbing rumours they had heard regarding the mistreatment of POWs in railway camps in northern Thailand.

As they were also able to move about relatively freely, Gairdner decided to form a secret support group for the prisoners, which evolved into the 'V' organisation. Peter Heath volunteered and became an excellent fundraiser, with help from French, Danish and Swiss nationals in Bangkok. He also coordinated communication with camp leaders. They soon enlisted the help of some Royal Army Service Corps (RASC) drivers, whose job was to transport Japanese officers to and from the railway camps. Boon Pong also became involved, of course, at enormous risk to himself and his family.

Monthly exchanges occurred from September 1942 until the end of the war, with the POWs providing details of camp locations, conditions and medical needs, while the 'V' organisation supplied world news, medications and money. In 1943, when the 'Speedo' period started, Gairdner arranged a loan of 12,000 ticals (Thai dollars) from private individuals in Bangkok to support the prisoners. This was collected in 20-tical notes, which was the highest denomination the Japanese allowed the POWs to use. The problem now was how to deliver this large pile of notes. Eventually, this was done by the cool Mrs Gairdner, who concealed the cash in a bag of tapioca flour, which she passed to the prisoners right in front of a Japanese guard.

Boon Pong's involvement with the prisoners was more consistent, if even riskier. He had two roles. The first, legitimate involvement was as one of several traders travelling by barge selling canteen goods to the camps on the lower reaches of the river. Even in this role, he had a reputation for having the fairest prices and the lowest profit margin. However, it was his second, undercover role as part of the 'V' organisation that was more important. Given his unquestioned access to the camps, he was able to distribute cash, drugs and even wireless batteries (nick-named 'canary seeds') to the camp commanding officers. For individual prisoners, he would also cash cheques and advance money against any personal valuables they still possessed. If the Japanese had discovered his secret, there is no doubt that he would have been questioned and tortured by the Kempeitai, the Japanese secret police, and then executed. Thankfully, they never did realise his clandestine activities.

Boon Pong also brought out regular reports on the camp conditions and death rates from the commanders, which were passed on to Peter Heath and then to Siegenthaler at the Swiss Consulate in Bangkok. Under the terms of the Geneva Convention, a state that was neutral in any conflict could be accorded the status of 'Protecting Power', which meant representing the interests of one warring state within the occupied territory of the other. Switzerland was that power in Thailand for the British and Commonwealth countries.

The Swiss consul, Walter Siegenthaler, was born in Lyss, Switzerland in July 1897. He moved to Bangkok in 1919 as a junior official in an import/export business, Diethelm and Co., and by 1934 was manager of the company. In June 1935, he was appointed the Swiss honorary consul to Siam, as it was then called. He had no idea that this appointment would be a pivotal moment in his life, and a critical one for the lives and well-being of thousands of POWs.

From the beginning of the war, under the terms of the Geneva Convention, neutral representatives of the Protecting Power, or the ICRC, could obtain lists of names and locations of POWs, provide relief supplies of food and clothing to the prisoners, and pay visits of inspection to the camps. In reality, these functions were continually opposed by the Japanese. Prime Minister Tojo said in 1942, 'where Japanese troops are facing hardships, there is no need to pamper POWs ... there's no knowing where this might end.'

As a result, particularly in southern Asia, it was difficult for the neutral agents to help the prisoners in any way. When an ICRC agent in Singapore complained about the treatment of prisoners, he was arrested and interrogated by the Japanese military police as a suspected spy. The message to the neutral representatives was clear. If they took too aggressive a stand, they ran the risk of both personal harm and jeopardising any relief getting to the prisoners.

This did not deter the untiring Herr Siegenthaler. In July 1942, he was able to inform the British authorities for the first time that 3,000 prisoners were working to build roads in the Ban Pong area. By April 1943, he was able to provide them with a list of the River Kwai camp sites. In June 1943, he provided reports of the terrible physical condition of many prisoners who had been sent to base hospitals from the jungle camps, as well as outlining their limited medical care. Through Siegenthaler, a strong diplomatic protest was made over these conditions; however, the Japanese simply said that the reports were untrue.

When denial failed to appease the diplomats, they tried deception. Alfred 'Pop' Nellis, a British POW, gives an excellent account of one such episode:

About September 1943, about one hundred POWs based at Kanchanaburi were picked out by the [Japanese], chiefly because they looked fit and well. They were given British K.D. [khaki drill] clothing and boots, which they had to get dressed in. They were taken to a clean hut. Here the [Japanese] had placed tables and chairs, tablecloths on the tables, vases of flowers, fruit of all tropical description and laid out with knives, forks, spoons, cups and saucers. The POWs were told to sit down, but not to touch anything. Nippon orderlies then brought in plates laden with European food and placed them on the table in front of each POW. A series of photographs were then taken; when this had been done, the POWs were taken away, ordered to undress and return the clothes they had been issued back to the stores. They were then sent back to work without even having partaken of one small scrap of food, only just having the chance of a good smell.

Siegenthaler remained determined to provide some relief to the prisoners. He met with the Japanese Chargé d'Affaires at their Bangkok embassy in March and in June of 1943 to request permission to do so. Again, he was met with refusal. The Japanese were afraid that allowing relief packages would be an admission that the rations they were providing the prisoners were insufficient. They were also worried that any provision of relief would be used as propaganda.

Siegenthaler would not give up. Eventually, the Japanese agreed to his requests – initially only allowing him access as a private individual. An American State Department report summarises the situation well:

Despatch 775, April 3 1944, from Bern, reported the substance of an oral communication to Walter Siegenthaler, Swiss Consul at Bangkok, by a spokesman of the Japanese Embassy, as follows: The Japanese authorities do not recognize the Swiss Consulate at Bangkok as representing American and British interests in Thailand, and therefore gratuities to prisoners of war should be made to Mr. Siegenthaler in his private capacity. Receipts for relief parcels and pocket money would henceforth be signed by the Japanese Commandant and not, as before, by camp authorities and senior British Officers. Finally, the Japanese authorities do not recognize the representative of the International Red Cross Committee in Thailand.

In 1944, Siegenthaler was finally allowed access to the prisoners on behalf of Britain. By late 1944, he was spending 11,500 pounds sterling per quarter on behalf of the British authorities. This money purchased a large variety of foods and condensed milk, soap, toilet paper, cigarettes and pipe tobacco, medicines, boots and other clothing items. Sadly, it seems that little of these supplies reached the prisoners. The majority was looted by the Japanese camp commandants, with many of these supplies being discovered in hiding places at the end of the war. Still, the small amount given to the POWs undoubtedly saved some lives, while also reminding them that they were not forgotten.

For Don's survival, however, Siegenthaler's most important contribution came in ensuring that camp inspections took place. Once again, the Japanese initially refused to recognise the right of Protecting Power representatives to do so; however, they eventually agreed to issue a limited number of permits for neutral representatives to inspect select base hospitals and camps, if numerous conditions were followed. For example, advance notice had to be provided. This period of time was used to superficially improve the appearance of the camp, which the POWs called a 'show camp'. The inspectors were also warned not to anger the camp authorities by referring to humanitarian texts and agreements.

A post-war report from the ICRC committee gives a good summary of how the visits were conducted:

> The duration of the visit was generally restricted to two hours, made up of one for a conversation with the camp commandant, thirty minutes for visiting quarters, and thirty minutes for an interview, in the presence of the Japanese officers of the camp, with a camp leader appointed by them. No communication with the other prisoners was authorised, and negotiations undertaken with the object of altering this state of things were not successful. The camp commandants often refused to reply to questions put to them.

After the war, some ex-POWs directly or implicitly criticised the ICRC/Protecting Power representatives who were able to visit the camps, alleging that they accomplished nothing with the Japanese authorities. This is unfair and untrue. They were regarded with suspicion and ill-will by the Japanese, after all, and were sometimes afraid for their own safety. They also learned that an Allied commanding officer who openly criticised conditions was liable to be beaten after their departure. To avoid this, the officer sometimes conveyed the true situation to the inspector by passing a written message while shaking hands. These inspectors put their lives on the line. And, as already detailed, one unauthorised communication probably saved my father's life.

10 WEARY DUNLOP

TARSAU, OCTOBER-DECEMBER, 1943

Within a few weeks of receiving his secret supply of vitamins, Don's medical condition improved significantly. The swelling in his legs disappeared. The numbness in his hands and feet was much improved, and he had much less pain, so he could sleep better. Most importantly, coordination and some strength had returned to his leg muscles, meaning he could walk again.

At the same time, another remarkable event occurred – the completion of the Death Railway. On 17 October 1943, the two stretches of rail – one travelling south-east from Burma, and the other north-west from Nong Pladuk – met at Konkoita amid deep jungle. The workers were 40km south of the Burma border and 262km from the Thai terminus.

The Japanese railway engineers were elated, and able to produce numerous statistics for their military supervisors. They stated that the completion of the line involved building four million cubic metres of earthwork, shifting three million cubic metres of rock, and the construction of 14km of bridgework. For these bridges, they had used 1,700 cubic metres of bridging timber and 18,400 cubic metres of timber poles. The blasting of cuttings had consumed about 300 tons of explosives. Four hundred elephants and their mahouts had supplemented the human toil.

One statistic is glaringly absent, however – the huge number of human lives lost and damaged by the construction. We will return to those shameful statistics later. However, one Japanese railway engineer, Yoshihiko Futamatsu, had the audacity to say in a post-war book: 'To use prisoners of war and with their cooperation to complete the task constituted a unique phenomenon in world railway construction.'

Unique indeed.

On 25 October 1943, at Konkoita, the Japanese conducted a formal ceremony to celebrate their achievement. The original plan was for Head of State Ba Maw from Burma and Prime Minister Phibunsongkhram from Thailand to ride the first train from either end of the line, greeting each other at the border between the two countries. This was abandoned due to fears of Allied air bombing, which was becoming a frequent occurrence. Instead, Lieutenant Colonel Sasaki, commanding officer of the Japanese Fifth Railway Regiment (responsible for the Burmese construction) and Lieutenant Colonel Imai, commanding officer of the Japanese Ninth Railway Regiment (responsible for the Thai construction) drove specially made gun-metal spikes into an ebony sleeper to finish construction. They then saluted the officer in overall control of the project, Major General Ishida Eiguma, and declared their task complete.

A locomotive, sporting the crossed flags of Japan and Thailand in front of the smokestack and pulling three railroad trucks carrying Japanese officers wearing their best khaki uniforms, advanced from the south-east to the junction point. Upon arrival, the Japanese Southern Army band played their national anthem. Engineer Futumatsu was one of many observers of the ceremony. In his memoir, he wrote, 'Even now, the inspiration of that moment is something I cannot forget.'

To mark the official opening of the railway, the prisoners in the jungle camps were given a day's holiday and a special issue of extra food, including fish, margarine and Japanese tinned milk. Some were even given an issue of cigarettes. At one camp (Kinsaiyok), the Japanese dynamited the river, allowing the POWs to have a celebration meal with over 100kg of fresh fish. The military band returning from Konkoita also made several stops at camps along the line, playing a selection of western and Japanese tunes to entertain prisoners and Japanese soldiers alike.

For the pleasure of the Japanese soldiers and Korean guards, a brothel train stopped at various camps along the river. When some of the women on the train saw how destitute the prisoners were, they passed them some cigarettes and a little cash. These sex workers, or 'comfort women', were mostly Korean or Chinese, including some young teenagers who had been kidnapped or coerced into sexual slavery by the Imperial Japanese Army. The provision of these military brothels, or 'comfort stations', for the satisfaction of the soldiers was endorsed by Emperor Hirohito.

This endorsement was likely given due to a horrifying incident from their recent past. In December 1937, Japanese troops in China began a six-week-long massacre which essentially destroyed the city of Nanking (now Nanjing). During this time, they raped between

20,000 and 80,000 Chinese women. This is still known today as 'The Rape of Nanking'. These mass rapes were condemned around the world. In the aftermath, the embarrassed emperor ordered the military to expand the supply of 'comfort stations' to look after his soldiers' sexual appetites.

During World War 2, tens of thousands of 'comfort women' were enslaved in these brothels. They were repeatedly raped by their captors under brutal, inhumane conditions, resulting in agonising pain, sexually trans-mitted diseases, pregnancies and often death. Records of this system of forced prostitution were destroyed after the war, and, for many years, Japan tried to downplay or even deny its existence. Finally, in 1993, after multiple protests from South Korea, the Japanese government acknowledged the atrocities. In December 2015, it formally apologised and announced that it would give financial reparations to the few surviving Korean comfort women, as well as to the families of those who had died. Some of the women rejected the Japanese payment, asking for a larger compen-sation payment and a stronger apology. At the time of writing, Japan has refused to meet their demands.

In honour of the completion of the railway, the Japanese leaders also decided that religious ceremonies would be held at the jungle camps, to honour those who had died during the building of the railway. In some cases, large inscribed crosses were erected at the cemeteries. At others, Japanese officers – dressed in their best uniforms and wearing ceremonial swords – laid wreaths at the graves of prisoners. None of them acknowledged that they were the major reason why so many of these young men had died, of course. Many of the assembled prisoners turned away at the hypocrisy.

———

On the same day that the official celebration occurred, 25 October 1943, another event at Tarsau had a major beneficial effect on Don's survival. This was the arrival of the legendary Australian doctor Lieutenant Colonel (later Sir) Ernest Edward 'Weary' Dunlop to take charge of the hospital camp.

Born in Wangaratta, Victoria in 1907, he graduated from the University of Melbourne in 1934 in both pharmacy and medicine. A champion boxer and a good Australian Rules player, he also became famous as an international rugby union player. Under these circumstances, the nickname 'Weary' seems odd. In fact, it was a joking reference to his last name – a play on 'tired', like a Dunlop tyre.

Weary Dunlop

When the war began in 1939, he had been working as a surgeon in London but immediately enlisted in the Australian Army Medical Corps (AAMC) and the Australian Imperial Force (AIF). When war in the Pacific broke out, he was transferred – after distinguished service in the Middle East – to take command of a hospital in Java, in the Dutch East Indies, in February 1942. A month later, the island fell to the Japanese, and he and his fellow prisoners were transferred to Singapore. In January 1943, he became the commanding officer and chief physician of more than a thousand POWs sent to work on the Death Railway. This group became known as 'Dunlop Force', 'D Force' or 'Dunlop's Thousand'. He earned the loyalty and respect of his men through his compassionate, skilful medical care and his courage in standing up to the brutality of their Japanese captors.

When he took over at Tarsau, Dunlop was already aware of the dreadful conditions in the hospital camp, as well as the low morale among the men. He had visited the camp twice before, for a few days each time, and had been appalled by what he saw. On the second visit, he arrived in Tarsau by barge with a group of very sick patients, many of whom could not walk. No help was provided to move these men to the hospital. After waiting for hours, Dunlop literally took things into his own hands – he carried 19 of these immobile patients up the bank from the barge on his back.

Once based there, he was determined to improve matters at Tarsau. He had already identified many of the problems with the camp. These included a lack of segregation of patients, frequently resulting in cross-infection, as well as inadequate latrines and sanitation. There were not enough trained medical orderlies. There was a lack of hot water and medical supplies. The medical staff who were present were poorly organised. Hygiene inside the huts was unsatisfactory. Furthermore, the sick needed better food. To combat this problem, he decided to deduct more cash from the pay of officers and working men.

His first observation after arrival – in a secret diary that he kept during his imprisonment – was that the camp now had 'a formidable system of parades, with a great deal of time consumed in numbering and checking all the troops'. Presumably this was an attempt to keep the prisoners busy, since, with the railway complete, it – and the service road running parallel – only needed occasional maintenance work. He also noted that 'the hospital today obtained some most valuable drugs and money.' To preserve his safety, he did not write the name of the supplier. However, he later clarified that it was 'by grace of that magnificent man, Boon Phong [sic]'.

The next day, it was decided that Dunlop would take charge of the hospital and convalescent depot, while the other senior doctor, Lieutenant Colonel Harvey, would do all official liaison work with the Japanese camp author-ities. Soon, Dunlop was demanding, and obtaining, significant improvements. These included the construc-tion of fresh, deep and covered latrines, along with the provision of oil lamps for illumination when men used the latrines at night. He appointed masters in each ward to be responsible for hygiene and to ensure the removal of contamination by 9 a.m. each day. He also instigated the rebuilding of defective and leaning huts, as well as the erecting of clothes lines between wards. Carpenters became busy making more bamboo stretchers, leg splints, artificial limbs, backrests for beds and crutches. A school was also established to train more medical orderlies.

As previously mentioned, the huts were crawling with bugs, the blankets infested with lice. To combat this, a fumigation hut was built, enabling all blankets and bedding to be fumigated systematically. The existing benches in the huts were dismantled, and each bamboo slat passed through fire to destroy the bugs and their eggs. Extra four-gallon cans were also procured to ensured that, at every mess point where meals were served, there was boiling water for the sterilisation of mess gear before food was eaten. Another order made by Dunlop was that every man able to walk had to bathe in the river each day. Thankfully this group now included my dad. With the 'Speedo' era now behind them, the Japanese leaders also allowed the prisoners to have periods of rest (*'yasume'*).

This succession of small changes had a big overall effect. Living conditions were much improved. Prisoners moved about briskly and with more purpose. There was an obvious lift in morale in the whole camp – all due to Dunlop's interventions.

———

In addition to maintaining a diary (a practice banned by the Japanese), Dunlop kept other contraband, including maps and a compass. However, he had one other secret item which was even more precious: a wireless radio set. This ensured that Dunlop and his fellow POWs could keep up to date with the progress of the war by listening to news from the BBC and other radio services. Discovery of the set would have meant torture and execution for those involved. To avoid detection after use, the radio would be quickly disassembled and the parts hidden among the packs and kit of Dunlop and a few trusted friends. It would then be reassembled for use when the Korean/Japanese guards were no longer around. Miraculously, it was never discovered over the course of Dunlop's three and a half years of captivity – but the closest call was at Tarsau.

The Kempeitai functioned much like Hitler's Gestapo but had even broader authority to act. In fact, they had almost complete autonomy and sweeping powers, including the right to arrest, assault, torture and execute defiant POWs. Their reputation for cruelty was well deserved.

On 5 November 1943, at Tarsau, they arrested Weary Dunlop. Some of his fellow officers had been questioned and beaten over the previous couple of days on the suspicion of having a radio. Now it seemed it was Dunlop's turn to be interrogated about it.

After his arrest, Dunlop was thrown into a small cell. To his horror, in a concealed pocket of his shirt, he found notes that he had written detailing the latest wireless news. Before the *kempei* returned, the notes were chewed up and swallowed.

For the next four hours, he was subjected to a steady interrogation but remained adamant that he knew nothing. At this point, the interrogating officer changed his tactics. He screamed that they knew all about Dunlop and his radio set and told him that he would be executed. First, however, he would be made to talk.

Two soldiers clapped him in manacles and beat him with pieces of firewood each time his answer to a question was unsatisfactory. Eventually, his interrogator said that he had run out of patience. Now Dunlop would die.

Dunlop was pushed to a nearby tree, where the manacles were used to tie his wrists behind it. This left his bare belly exposed to an execution squad of four soldiers with fixed bayonets.

The officer began a countdown of 30 seconds, while the soldiers worked themselves up with blood-curdling yells and belly grunts. With 10 seconds to go, Dunlop was asked if he had a last message for his relatives.

'Conveyed by thugs like you? No thanks,' he replied.

As the countdown concluded, the soldiers drew back their bayonets for the fatal thrust. The officer's face reddened and he raised a hand to stop them, explaining how Dunlop must suffer more before he died.

He received a heavy beating before being pushed back into a cell. Some hours later, he was tied to the same tree, given the same countdown as the cold steel of the bayonets aimed at his exposed belly – only to again receive the last-second reprieve.

This time, he was led to a metal-framed pen, which contained a Thai prisoner. The next evening, Dunlop's companion was removed from the pen and shot. Dunlop assumed that he would be next, thinking that at least this would be a better means of execution.

His *kempei* interrogator confronted him one more time. When he again denied any knowledge of a radio set, he was told, to his amazement, that he would be released. He was given beer and cigarettes and asked not to have hard feelings against the Kempeitai. The interrogating officer, who Dunlop nicknamed 'Stone Face' due to his lack of facial expression, said: 'We *kempei* do but do our duty.'

After the end of the war, Dunlop saw 'Stone Face' again in an identification parade of possible war criminals. Amazingly, in a spirit of forgiveness, Dunlop refused to identify his tormentor.

11 ANOTHER CHRISTMAS IN CAPTIVITY

TARSAU, NOVEMBER–DECEMBER 1943

In the last two months of 1943, having recovered from beriberi, Don found himself in the convalescent unit of Tarsau hospital camp. His diet was significantly better. In addition to the inevitable rice, most meals were now supplemented with small quantities of meat stew, beans and sometimes an egg. This would be accompanied by sweet tea. However, because of chronic dysentery and an inability to properly absorb the nutrients in the food, he could not gain weight.

Standards of hygiene, both in food preparation and in the hospital wards, also slowly improved after Dunlop's orders. In spite of this, there was another outbreak of cholera in November, though it was relatively well contained. Still, there were about 40 cases in total, with about three-quarters of these men dying.

In late November, after repeated requests, the Japanese supplied the hospital with 250 hemp rice sacks, 200 fibre-type rice mats, and 300 other mats. These were supplied as blankets to the neediest men, with the sickest getting priority. The new 'blankets' were very welcome.

The weather was also much better, as the rainy season was mercifully over. The days were warm and fine, while the nights were cool. This undoubtably improved morale. Still, it became obvious to the Allied officers that more could be done in this regard. Increasing recreation and entertainment activities at Tarsau should be more of a priority, for example. A meeting on this subject was held on 22 November. At this meeting, it was decided that the expanded activities should include concerts and other performances, quizzes and competitions, as well as arts and crafts programmes, which would be specially targeted towards limbless men. There would also be education activities, lectures, classes and public readings, as books were scarce.

Officers were nominated to coordinate each programme. The officer in charge of education and library activities was Major E.W. Swanton. He was a great authority on cricket, it turned out, and entertained the men on several evenings with his many sports stories. After the war, he became famous in Britain as a cricket commentator on BBC Radio, as well as a cricket correspondent for the *Daily Telegraph*.

As Christmas 1943 approached, a special effort was made to give the prisoners the best possible time under the circumstances. The officers and the few working men agreed to donate extra money from their wages to be spent on Christmas meals, gifts, cigarettes and money donations to those in greatest need. There was a general mood of optimism that this might be their last Christmas in captivity. The news from the hidden wireless set told them that the Germans and Japanese were on the retreat, while Italy had officially capitulated to the Allies on 3 September 1943. Surely Allied victory was not far away?

This belief was reinforced when Allied bombers began flying over Tarsau at night. Because of the cold nights, the prisoners had previously been allowed to light fires in the open spaces between huts. This was especially helpful to the ulcer patients, as the cold air worsened their pain levels. Some chose to sleep outdoors all night, close to the fires. On 17 December 1943, however, the Japanese commander ordered new air raid precautions. If Allied planes were heard approaching, all fires and lights were to be extinguished, and all POWs who were sleeping outside were to return to their huts. They were not even allowed to smoke in the huts. The obvious fear shown by the Japanese delighted the prisoners.

On Christmas Eve 1943, a formal memorial service for the combined British, Australian, Dutch and Japanese dead was held. Tarsau had three cemeteries (see map), one of which was solely for cholera victims, and identified only as cemetery no. 3, while the others were named St George's and St Luke's. Already, they held over 800 graves. All the Japanese officers and Allied prisoners gathered near the cemeteries and raised a large cross and dais. Two wreaths were laid on the cross to honour casualties from the Japanese and Allied armies. The new Japanese camp commander praised the prisoners for their work in building the railroad and helping to achieve a Greater East Asia. Despite this hypocrisy, the men appreciated the subsequent religious service, conducted mainly by Padre Alcock. The camp seemed to be filled with the spirit of Christianity, they felt, and a general surge of optimism.

Christmas Day 1943 found almost all the men in good spirits. In the morning, they were greeted by carol singing in many parts of the camp. The Japanese did not provide any extra food rations but, thanks to additional cash donations to the canteen fund, a few food extras were available. However, Dunlop was disappointed

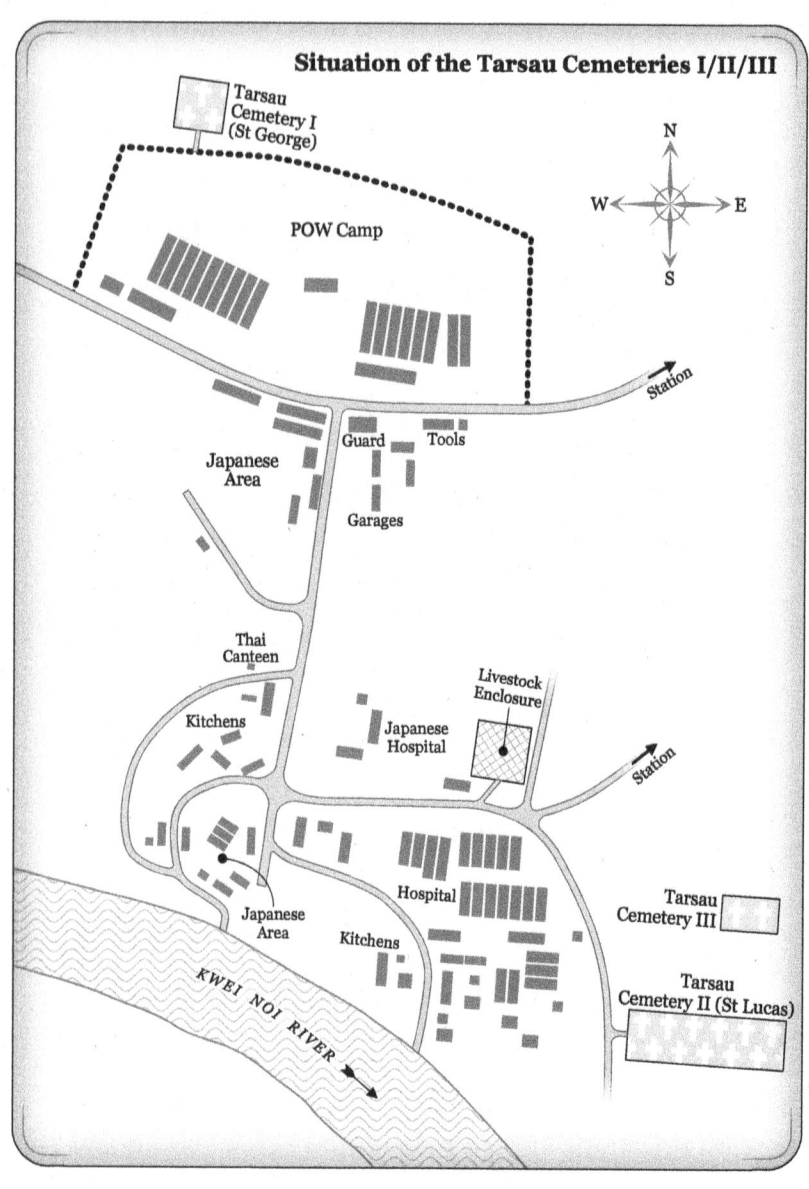

Situation of the Tarsau Cemeteries I/II/III

Tarsau Cemetery I (St George)

POW Camp

N
W E
S

Station

Japanese Area

Guard Tools

Garages

Thai Canteen

Kitchens

Livestock Enclosure

Japanese Hospital

Station

Japanese Area

Kitchens

Hospital

Tarsau Cemetery III

Tarsau Cemetery II (St Lucas)

KWEI NOI RIVER

with these, calling them a 'flop', and expressing concern about 'suspected kitchen racketeers'. The Japanese were not the only enemies the sick men had to contend with, it seemed.

In the afternoon, the camp was treated to an excellent production of the pantomime *Cinderella*. It was performed on a little stage built of bamboo in front of all the prisoners and most of the Japanese officers. Excellent dresses and costumes were made using mosquito netting and other scraps of cloth, aluminium foil, tinsel and various oddments. The audience gasped when the curtain swung back to reveal the elegantly dressed 'ladies'. However, any doubt about the gender of these 'females' could be resolved by looking at the obvious scabies and ulcer scars on their legs.

In the evening, Santa Claus (Captain Vardy, one of the medical officers), complete with red and white uniform and flowing white beard, visited the wards. Various others performed comedy sketches and acrobatics in the concert area. Lotteries were held in each hut, with prizes including small amounts of cash and a few bars of soap. Overall, it was a memorable day and a great tribute to the resilience of these remarkable men.

One other pleasant surprise occurred before the end of the year. Boon Pong arrived at Tarsau on 30 December by barge, delivering a valuable supply of drugs, as well as 3,000 ticals from the Swiss consul. Some of this money was used to buy medication, including iodoform and phenol, from another river trader – medication that Dunlop regarded as being invaluable for treating men with tropical ulcers. Fewer amputations would be needed now.

It was a small win, perhaps, but a win nonetheless.

12 MONOTONY

TARSAU, JANUARY–JUNE 1944

The new year was ushered in with quiet revelry by the prisoners. Some Scottish Gordon Highlanders had planned a more raucous, Hogmanay-style celebration, having somehow manufactured a still with the intent of producing some alcoholic spirits. However, their plan was discovered by a British officer, and, as they were using valuable hospital vegetables to make the brew, the still and spirits were confiscated. Much to their disgust, the alcohol was instead used for medical purposes.

In the huts, the men sang some nostalgic songs. No doubt Don sang his favourite party piece, 'Molly Malone', in memory of his Dublin roots. There was time now for him to reflect on the horrors of the preceding year. He had endured mosquito-infested jungle, the construction of the Wampo viaduct and the torture of the 'Speedo' period. He had been severely traumatised by seeing the ravages of cholera at close quarters, even having to help construct a mass grave. He had suffered from malaria, beriberi and dysentery, and remained malnourished and emaciated. However, at least he had survived.

Nora was always in his thoughts and prayers. He worried about her health, about how she was coping with wartime stress. Even though the war with Japan had now entered its third year, he had not yet received any of the letters she had written to him, although this was not unusual for Allied soldiers in the jungle camps. Mail from Ireland had first to be sent to Britain, then by ship to Vladivostok in Siberia, as Russia was not at war with Japan at that time. Letters would often remain there for months before being sent to Tokyo. Here, there was a significant shortage of qualified interpreters to act as censors, which resulted in a further backlog. After censorship, letters to POWs in Japan and some other occupied territories, such as Hong Kong, had a good chance of being delivered to the prisoners. In Thailand, however, there were major logistical problems in delivering any letter to the appropriate camp.

There were similar difficulties for the prisoners in writing home. For one thing, letters were not allowed.

Instead, on an unpredictable basis, they were issued post-cards that could be filled in and mailed to their loved ones. These allowed an individual prisoner to state which country he was interned in, that his health was excellent, usual or poor, or that he was ill in hospital. He could say that he was working for pay, or not working. The final entry read, 'Please see that ... is taken care [of].' Unfortunately, none of the cards from my father to my mother (she received two or three during the entire war) have survived, but one from his brother Dick has lasted. It was written on 24 August 1943 to their parents, saying that he was in Taiwan, that his health was excellent, and asking for prayers for 'my life and welfare'.

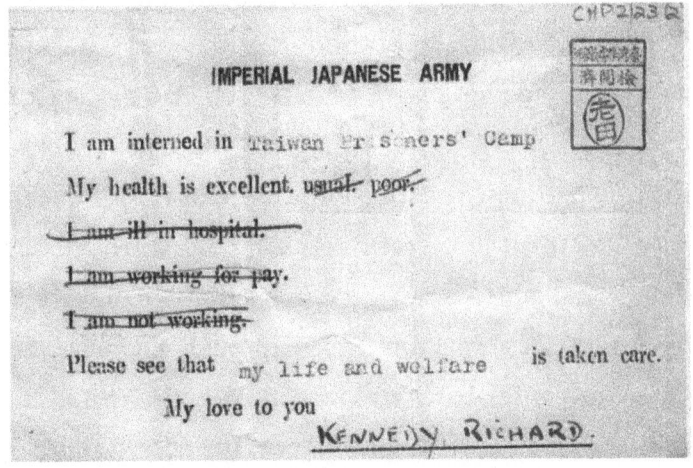

Dick's postcard home

A colleague of Don's decided to be more informative about the terrible food in his postcard, writing 'lousy grub' in the space provided. When questioned about this, he assured a Japanese censor that this was the name of his aunt. He was issued a new card, which he rewrote, reading: 'Please see that Auntie Lousy Grub is taken care of.'

Don had no knowledge of the health of his ageing parents in Dublin, neither that his mother had suffered a debilitating stroke in February 1944. Likewise, he was totally unaware that his brother Dick, who had left Singapore before him, was now imprisoned in a mining camp in Taiwan. Neither did he know that his brother Dermot, a surgeon, had joined the British Royal Army Medical Corps (RAMC) as a lieutenant in July 1942 and was stationed with the British forces in North Africa.

Thanks to Dunlop's secret radio set, Dad did at least have some general knowledge of the war. He knew that the tide had now turned significantly in favour of the Allies. German forces were retreating in North Africa, in Italy and on the Eastern Front. An invasion of France, to open a Western Front, was expected. Likewise, he knew how the Japanese navy had been decimated by the American Pacific Fleet, and how the Americans had begun advancing northwards from one island group to the next in the Central Pacific. Yet the Japanese still had control of most of their new empire: large parts of China, Formosa (Taiwan), Hong Kong, Thailand, Malaya, the East Indies, the Philippines and almost all of Burma.

Don and his fellow prisoners could dream of liberation, but realistically knew that, if it were to happen, it was still some time away.

———

What about the effect of the now-completed railway, built at such human cost? Japanese Colonel Takeo Kurahashi gave a succinct summary: 'Although the importance of the completed railroad was very great from the standpoint of supply for Burma, and although the Burma area Army entertained great hopes for it, the anticipated capacity failed to materialise.'

This shortfall in capacity speaks to the biggest problem with the railway, especially in the first eight months of operation: the terrible quality of its construction. There were two reasons for this. Obviously, the POWs made no effort to ensure good construction, and were happy to do some sabotage whenever they could. Second, the Japanese engineers had been under severe pressure to complete their task as fast as possible, and therefore were not always able to closely supervise the work. They were focused on speed of construction, not durability. As a result, cuttings were sometimes barely wide enough to let a train pass, sleepers sank into the foundations in places, and many of the bridges hastily built with green timber were on the verge of collapse. Sleepers were often not even regularly laid and were compared to 'so many matches laid down by a giant hand'. One POW described how, at times, the rails would be up in the air above the sleepers, while at other times the sleeper would be up in the air with the rail attached. All this was before natural obstacles like landslides also began to damage the track.

There were numerous derailments. Bridges and curves on the track had to be negotiated at dead-slow speeds. Sometimes trains could only negotiate gradients that had been built more steeply than specified in the plans by getting their human cargo to disembark and walk to the next station.

The initial Japanese goal was that the Thailand–Burma railway would carry 6,000 tons of cargo each day (3,000 tons in each direction). When the railway was completed and the problems were identified, this goal was reduced to 1,000 tons daily. Ultimately, even this proved impossible. In the first full month of operation,

November 1943, only 45 trains made the journey. During the first six months of 1944, the railroad still only averaged two trains per day, or about 400 tons of cargo. This state of affairs amused and delighted the prisoners.

These supply issues were extremely detrimental to the Japanese war effort. However, they were not reported to military headquarters in Tokyo. Consequently, when the generals decided to invade northern India in early 1944 (the U-Go Offensive) – an offensive that Prime Minister Tojo gave formal final approval for while having a bath – he remained none the wiser about the rail issue. In fact, when he asked a staff officer if the supply situation was satisfactory, he was told that it was. After this assurance, he put his seal on the document ordering the attack.

The U-Go Offensive began on 6 March 1944, when three divisions of Japanese troops crossed from Burma into northern India, where they were met with fierce resistance from British and Indian troops. The battle continued for three months, even after the onset of monsoon rains. The reality for the Japanese army, however, was that they were incapable of supplying their soldiers with reinforcements, war material or even food on a reliable basis. As anticipated, this was true on sea or in the air, where the Allies were overwhelmingly dominant – but it was also true of road and rail, in large part due to the deficiencies of the Thailand–Burma Railway.

In June 1944, the diseased and starving Japanese troops began to retreat into northern Burma. More than half of their initial force of 115,000 men were dead or wounded. It was their greatest defeat to date in the Pacific War. Unknowingly, the Death Railway prisoners had made their contribution to the war effort.

————

Back at the Tarsau camp, in early January 1944 there were still just under 5,000 prisoners. Dunlop's diary records that 1,608 men were rated as 'fit', while 3,367 were sick. The death rates, while still unacceptable, were improving. Between 1 April 1943 and 29 December 1943, 676 men had died in Tarsau, but 'only' 50 of these deaths had been in December 1943, and the number was down to four in the first week of January 1944 – a new record. Dunlop attributed most of this success, if it can be so called, to an improved diet for the sick men. He recorded that better-quality rice and vegetables were being delivered by the Japanese trains, and dietary extras were being purchased thanks to extra cash provided by the Swiss legation and Boon Pong. Another 5,000 ticals was delivered in January.

At this point, word was received that the Tarsau hospital camp was to be closed over the following several months, the men to be moved by train, with the fittest of them returning to Singapore. They did not yet know that this was in preparation for them to be shipped to Japan to resume slave labour.

Sick men, including Don, would gradually be moved to six main base hospital camps near the southern start of the railway. These were a new camp called Nakom Paton, with 10,000 beds, as well as five existing camps at Nong Pladuk, Tamuang, Kanchanaburi, Tamarkan and Chungkai. The sick men were graded according to their level of infirmity. 'Heavy sick' patients would go to Nakom Paton and 'light sick' patients to Chungkai.

At this time, Don – while still unwell – was not classified in either of these categories, which resulted in him remaining at Tarsau for another five months. This proved a bit of a mixed blessing. While it meant that he was less likely to be shipped to Japan, the food and medical care was never as good in Tarsau as in the base camps.

Lieutenant Colonel Dunlop left Tarsau on 17 January 1944, bringing a group of 200 men to Chungkai by train. He left behind a hospital camp that was much better organised than when he came, with much improved hygiene and sanitation. Death rates were also much improved, and men were more optimistic that they would survive and not need limb amputations. What he did not leave behind, however, was his radio. So once again my dad and his fellow prisoners were cut off from news of the outside world.

Life at the Tarsau camp settled into a less stressful, if somewhat dull routine. Occasionally, work parties were still organised to do maintenance work or repairs on the railway or service road.

Outside of this, the prisoners saw little of the Japanese leadership. Most immediate contact with their captors was with the Korean guards. These Koreans were usually unwilling conscripts, although a few were volunteers enticed by pay of 50 yen per month, which was substantially more than a private in the Japanese army. Typically, the Koreans were organised in platoons of a dozen guards, with a Japanese junior officer and/or NCO theoretically in charge. In reality, the guards had a fair degree of autonomy by this point and were effectively in control of the POWs. Their job was to maintain discipline in the workforce, ensuring that they did not slacken in their work, commit acts of subordination nor try to escape.

The guards were often poorly treated by the Japanese. Some in turn took out their resentments on the prisoners, persecuting or beating them for little reason. Others stole supplies meant for the POWs and sold them on the black market. Many just followed orders, inflicting cruelty on the weakened men when there was no benefit in doing so.

On rare occasions, a few guards were sympathetic and friendly toward the prisoners. They secretly disliked the Japanese, seeing their commands as unreasonable. Sometimes they were even prepared to bend or break the rules in favour of the POWs. In Tarsau, Don and his mates came to know and like one particular guard known as 'Joe'. He stood out because he was at least six feet tall and was always happy and friendly. On one occasion, he went missing for several days. Later, the prisoners learned that Joe had been in prison. It turned out that the Japanese had discovered that he was stealing salt and other precious commodities from their stores and passing them on to sick prisoners.

The number of patients and prisoners in Tarsau steadily decreased in the first half of 1944, the Japanese plan being to empty the camp of Allied POWs by the end of April 1944. This did not happen. Instead, Don and a dwindling number of prisoners remained behind, watching many of their friends leave for hospital camps downriver, or, if healthy, for Singapore.

The records for the Tarsau hospital camp make for

sombre reading. Between November 1942 and the official closure in April 1944, 15,029 young men were treated in the hospital. Of these, 806 died and were buried in the camp.

Finally, in June 1944, Don was informed that – after a stay of 10 months – he was to leave Tarsau. When he arrived, he had been critically ill with advanced beriberi and had been unable to walk. Hospital conditions and Japanese work demands had been appalling. Now he was mobile, there was little work, and he could even bathe in the river Khwae Noi.

Still, even by the lax Japanese standards, he could not be described as healthy. He was 6 feet 1 inch tall and yet weighed only six stone (84 pounds or 38kg). Despite the improvement in food and medical supplies, he could still not gain weight. In fact, he looked skeletal.

His mental stress was also considerable. He was cut off from news of the outside world, the progress of the war, and the health of his fiancée and family. He had also had no contact with his friends in 'D' Battalion for almost a year.

Yet, somehow, he retained optimism that better days were ahead, and that this horrible war and imprisonment might soon end, even as he knew nothing about his next camp destination except its name: Tamuang.

13 FAREWELL TO THE JUNGLE

TAMUANG, JUNE–SEPTEMBER 1944

Don Kennedy was finally transferred to Tamuang on 14 June 1944. He and his fellow prisoners were perhaps the last patients to leave Tarsau hospital. At least they were able to travel in a more leisurely fashion than on previous moves – this time by train, on the same railway tracks they had helped to build. Their southbound journey was just under 100km long, from the 130km marker to the 39km post on the railway. After 21 months, Don was leaving the jungle behind. Fortunately for him, he would never return.

The men travelled in relative comfort in a long, heavy train that was pulled by a locomotive which burned logs instead of coal. Given that this reduced the locomotive's power and ability to haul the train's weight, as well as to overcome some poorly calculated gradients, the prisoners were made aware that they might be ordered to disembark from the train and push it up hills and around bends. They worried that, thanks to their own sabotage with sleepers and bridge construction, a train derailment could happen. They also had to worry about air attacks, which were becoming more frequent.

Luckily, nothing of this nature happened on their journey. Don was able to admire the beautiful scenery bordering the River Kwai, the completed viaduct at Wampo he had helped to build and the lush farmland around Kanchanaburi. While they were close geographically, Tamuang was a world away from Tarsau. He faced the change with some apprehension but much anticipation.

Tamuang was about 11km south of the town of Kanchanaburi. The camp was located near a small railway siding, easily recognised by a brilliant flame tree near the entrance. The site had originally been a tobacco plantation. When Don arrived, there were multiple newly constructed and neatly laid-out huts for a capacity of up to 10,000 men. There were hospital facilities for Allied prisoners, but also a Japanese hospital for their wounded and ill soldiers. Unlike in the jungle, there were plenty of doctors and medical orderlies to care for the POWs, and they even had some basic medical supplies.

Dad was overjoyed upon his arrival to be reunited with many of his old friends from Singapore, the FMSVF and 'D' Battalion. For example, he soon discovered that Stanley Pavillard would once again be providing him with medical care. He told Don how he had only recently recovered from a severe, life-threatening bout of typhus – an infectious disease contracted when a person is bitten by fleas or lice that have previously fed on rats. This disclosure likely would have had my dad wondering if perhaps Tamuang was not as clean as it appeared.

The camp had a wireless radio receiver, meaning an end to the complete isolation from world affairs that Don had experienced in Tarsau since January 1944. He learned some big news about the war: the Allies had made a successful landing in Normandy, France on D-Day, 6 June 1944, to open a second front in Europe. The Germans were now retreating on both the Western and Eastern Fronts. Many felt that the war in Europe could be over by the end of the year. It was also known that the Japanese were in retreat in Burma and on the southern Pacific islands. This gave the men a huge boost in morale.

The radio receiver was cleverly built inside a drinking water bottle and was never detected during frequent searches by the Japanese. It was only used late at night to pick up world news and always for short periods. The information received was released gradually to the prisoners over the next few days. In this way, it could be claimed that it came as a rumour supplied by a Thai trader on the river. It also prevented too many men from appearing jubilant at the same time, which might have triggered a search.

The radio required a heavy supply of current, and this was supplied by small torch batteries – though these did not last long. Some of these were obtained through Boon Pong, while the rest were supplied unknowingly by the Japanese. These were given to the Allied doctors for instruments such as an ophthalmoscope (for eye examinations), or an otoscope (for ear examinations). At one point, Pavillard recounted, the Japanese did become suspicious about the large number of batteries the doctors were requesting for such a small number of instruments. Some flattery saved the day. The doctors told the authorities that, undoubtedly, the best battery in the world was Japanese; in contrast, these Thai batteries that the doctors used were much inferior, running out of power quickly. This explanation was not true, of course, but it more than satisfied the investigators.

For Don, life at Tamuang settled into a fairly comfortable routine. The Japanese called *tenko* twice and sometimes three times a day, but otherwise the prisoners were left alone.

With the area having previously been a tobacco plantation, several plants were still growing. Soon, the more resourceful of the men developed a lucrative business rolling cigars for sale. Rolling the cigars was usually delegated to the large number of amputees in the camp, and this proved excellent occupational therapy for these unfortunate men. Likewise, tobacco grown in the surrounding countryside was purchased, then dried and shredded, before being sold in the canteen for cigarette rolling. A month's supply of this tobacco (sometimes referred to as 'Granny's Armpit') would cost a man about 65 cents, while a two-inch cigar cost two cents. The earnings from this enterprise were put into the canteen funds.

The men also set up a makeshift library. Quite a few of the prisoners had managed to hold on to a book or two during their captivity, so these were pooled and passed around. The Japanese commander then decided that these books should be censored. However, none of the so-called censors could understand English, so they simply stamped them with some Japanese characters and gave them back.

In the evening, for devout Catholic prisoners like Don, there was one more commitment: daily mass. This was celebrated by one of the chaplains in the camp, Fr Burke, a determined Redemptorist priest, who said mass in the open air near some bushes on the outskirts of the camp. This location had the added benefit of allowing some of the Catholic Korean guards to attend without being reprimanded by their officers. I'm sure this daily service gave my father great comfort and consolation in those dreary days.

It was not just the POWs who were looking to improve their days in the camp. The Japanese officers and their guards at one point decided to improve their nutrition by raising ducks. They put about 2,000 of these in a large pen which surrounded a pool, guarding them day and night to prevent the prisoners from stealing them. Fortunately, these guards were not vigilant; for example, after meals they tended to fall asleep under a nearby mango tree. Some POWs would then sneak into the pen and a few unfortunate ducks would meet an early demise. This tasty treat was a welcome addition to the prisoners' bland diet, which still consisted mainly of rice, a few added vegetables and some salted fish.

As previously mentioned, up to this point the POWs had not been kept in the camps by means of perimeter walls or barbed wire. In late 1944, however, there was a drastic change in this approach at Tamuang, as well as at all the other base camps on the Death Railway. The prisoners were ordered to build deep ditches surrounding each camp. These were 10 feet wide and 15 feet deep, complemented by some machine gun emplacements.

However, the purpose of these ditches was not to prevent escape. Instead, they were built because the Japanese were becoming increasingly fearful of an Allied landing or attack. The prisoners were told by sympathetic Korean guards that, if this happened, the men would be forced into the ditches and massacred.

They had potentially dug their own graves.

14 HELL SHIPS

TAMUANG AND TARDEN, SEPTEMBER–DECEMBER 1944

In early September 1944, the Japanese announced that 2,000 of the 'fittest' men in the Tamuang camp were to be sent to Japan. This news was received with considerable trepidation by the prisoners, as they knew that many Japanese ships were being sunk every month by the dominant American navy. Still, they had no choice but to comply.

In reality, none of the POWs could be deemed fit. They were all extremely underweight, most had ongoing symptoms of malaria, and many had dysentery and vitamin deficiency. Their captors also knew that some of these men would not survive the voyage, even if their ship was not sunk. The Japanese simply did not care. Their only priority was to fill the quotas needed to provide slave labour for industries in Japan. The weary prisoners were simply assembled and lined up, and a Japanese officer performed a quick visual inspection. The selection process often seemed arbitrary, but the decision was final. Medical officers were not allowed to appeal.

Unsurprisingly, Don was still too weak to be selected, but 124 of his colleagues from 'D' battalion were chosen. It was decided that Brigadier Arthur Varley, the leader of the Australian forces at the fall of Singapore and a highly decorated World War 1 veteran, would be in command.

These men were sent by rail to Singapore. On 6 September 1944, they were part of a group of 2,300 POWs who boarded two 'hell ships', the *Rakuyo Maru* and *Kachidoki Maru*, which were scheduled to sail to Japan in a convoy of 13 ships, including two oil tankers and six escorting destroyers. The convoy was known as 'Japan Party 3'.

The 'hell ships' were so called by the POWs because of the horrific conditions on board. Up to a thousand prisoners could be crammed into the holds, and they were provided with little food, fresh water or appropriate sanitation. This might have been tolerable for a short journey, but the voyage from Singapore to Japan could take up to 70 days. Men died from dehydration, heat exhaustion and disease, as well as beatings and shootings by their captors. In addition, the Japanese never identified these ships as carrying Allied prisoners, leaving them vulnerable to attack by Allied submarines and ships. Historian Gregory Michno has estimated that over 19,000 POWs died as a result of Allied attacks on these hell ships (more than all the Allied deaths on the Death Railway), while 1,540 died from violence and conditions in the holds. Of the original 124 men from 'D' battalion, 105 were later listed as missing by the Japanese. Don and his colleagues in the camp would be unaware of the fate of most of their friends until the end of the war.

On 12 September 1944, Japan Party 3 was attacked by four US submarines in the Luzon Strait between the Philippines and Taiwan. The *Rakuyo Maru* was sunk by USS *Sealion*, and the *Kachidoki Maru* by USS *Pampanito*. Over 1,500 of the Allied prisoners died, including about 350 POWs already in lifeboats, who were killed when a Japanese vessel opened fire on them. Brigadier Varley did not survive.

However, about 150 survivors clinging to bits of wreckage and rafts were picked up by the American submarines and brought to the island of Saipan. After medical treatment, many of the Australian POWs were flown home in late October. For the first time since the

Asian war began, they were able to provide corroboratory first-hand details of the horrors they had endured on the Death Railway.

On 17 November 1944, in the Australian House of Commons, the Secretary of State for War, Sir James Grigg, and acting Prime Minister Forde made statements revealing the horrific conditions on the railway to the Australian public and the world at large. Sir James explained how 'the lowest estimate of deaths [was] one in five.' After outlining the horrors, parliament recommended that a copy of Grigg's statement should be sent 'to Dublin for the benefit of the Japanese consul-general who is residing in that city'.

For my mother back in Ireland, this news undoubtedly caused great alarm and anxiety. She would not have known that her fiancé had only narrowly avoided selection to travel on Japan Party 3. By now she had received one or perhaps two of the previously described POW postcards from Don, telling her that he was in a Siamese (Thai) camp. However, she was also aware that these cards were always several months out of date. So the question must have loomed large in her mind. Was Don among the dead referred to by the Australian government?

In Mallow, she leaned on her mother and sister for support. Her religious faith was also strong and she prayed daily to St Anthony. Somehow, she found reserves of strength and optimism, even as she experienced doubt and fear. She remained convinced that the man she loved would return to her and that, when the long nightmare ended, they would marry and build a life together.

———

Many of the trains arriving in Tamuang were now filled with badly wounded and sick Japanese troops from the battlefields in Burma. During their long journey south, these soldiers were not provided with any food or water. Furthermore, the trucks they travelled in were filthy, their wounds were often septic and they were rarely accompanied by a nurse – and never a doctor.

Working parties of Allied POWs would meet these trains and carry the wounded and sick to the Japanese hospital. Many of them were terrified to see European faces, perhaps for the first time in their lives, thinking they had fallen into enemy hands. They were also amazed when the white men tried to comfort them by giving them water and cigarettes. In contrast, their fellow Japanese guards and soldiers in Tamuang seemed indifferent to their suffering, as it was considered shameful to be wounded and stop fighting for the emperor. Many subsequently committed *hara-kiri* (ritual suicide with a sword) rather than returning to Japan and bringing disgrace to their families.

As for the other POWs, with the improved diet and much easier work demands, many of them had gained back some weight and well-being – and some even found that their sexual urges, dormant for so long, were returning. The local Thai ladies were happy to satisfy these urges, it turned out, in return for money, cigarettes or even woollen socks, which suddenly became a valuable commodity in the camp.

To enable these liaisons to occur, after dark, one or more long bamboo poles would be used as a bridge to cross the deep ditch surrounding the camp. However, the motives for crossing over the ditch were not always sinful; for example, Fr Burke sometimes sent men to purchase altar wine for mass from local suppliers. Whatever the reason, these crossings became ever more commonplace, to the point that sympathetic Catholic guards warned that the men should be more vigilant. They suspected that the Japanese authorities had become aware of these nightly excursions.

One night, just after midnight, the POWs were awakened by a bugle and agitated Korean guards running between huts, shouting '*tenko*'. The men were forced to parade as usual, with some of the sleepier prisoners being slapped and beaten when they forgot their Japanese numbers.

Suddenly a loud rifle shot rang out.

For at least another hour, they had to remain at attention in the parade area before being allowed to return to their huts. The POWs feared the worst.

The next morning, the Japanese confirmed that a prisoner, Fusilier D.W. Wanty, had been shot and killed 'while trying to escape'. During the prolonged *tenko*, he had been hastily buried, but Lieutenant Colonel Knights insisted that his body should be handed over for Christian burial. The Japanese reluctantly agreed, though this did not sate Knights' fury, promising that the perpetrator of this crime would face justice after the war.

He was true to his word. In June 1946, in Singapore, Major Totare Mizutani was found guilty of killing Wanty 'in violation of the laws and usages of war'. It turned out that Wanty had actually returned to camp while the search was ongoing and was found by Mizutani and a guard crouching 10 yards inside the camp perimeter. Mizutani ordered the guard to shoot him. When the guard refused, he did so himself. A report from a British medical officer showed that Wanty had been shot in the front, disproving the defence's claim that he had been running away. Mizutani was sentenced to death and executed by hanging.

———

By November 1944, it was apparent to the Japanese that they were steadily losing ground in Burma and that they needed to prepare for the efficient evacuation of their troops from Burma, as well as the defence of Thailand.

Once again, they began assembling work parties in the Railway base camps, mainly for the purpose of road construction. A group of 400 men was sent from Tamuang up to Wampo to build a road running westward to Tavoy on the coast of Burma. The nightmare of 'Speedo' work conditions began again for these men, aggravated by poor food and little or no medical support. Similarly, another 1,000 men were sent to build a road through a mountain pass between Prachuap in Thailand and Mergui in Burma, again with dreadful work conditions that resulted in the return of illness and multiple deaths.

My dad and others were sent to Tarden, about 50km north-west of Tamuang, to build a road to Tamarkan. The conditions were perhaps not as severe as the ones described above, but it should also be remembered that these men were among the weakest of the remaining prisoners. Don was in Tarden from 8 November to 2 December 1944, but I have no other details regarding his time building this road, nor of the conditions in the camp, which was presumably small and temporary.

When the road work was complete, he was moved again, this time to the large camp at Tamarkan. This camp was located close to two bridges, one wooden and one concrete, spanning the Mae Klong (Khwae Yai) River.

Don had no idea at the time that the nearby concrete bridge would one day become world famous. His home for the next three months would be situated next to the 'Bridge on the River Kwai'.

15 FRIENDLY FIRE

TAMARKAN, DECEMBER 1944–FEBRUARY 1945

Don and his fellow workers arrived in Tamarkan on 3 December 1944, after a hike of about 35km from Tarden in blazing heat. The camp was situated about 2km north of the town of Kanchanaburi. To get to it, the exhausted, emaciated and poorly clothed men had to cross a concrete and steel bridge north of the camp, one that spanned the Mae Klong, or Khwae Yai, river. It is hard for me to imagine that this was the same 'Bridge on the River Kwai' that I was to leisurely cross in the company of my wife, Maggie, and many other healthy, well-dressed tourists, more than 60 years later.

When the POWs arrived, they were told that their timing was fortuitous. Four days earlier, on the evening of 29 November 1944, an Allied bombing attack had caused death and destruction in the camp. The attack had been aimed at the two bridges that crossed the Mae Klong, as well as a Japanese anti-aircraft gun battery situated outside the camp. The bomber pilots had no idea that they might be harming soldiers from their own side, of course, since the Japanese refused to provide identification markers of hospitals or POW camps that could be seen from the air.

Australian Major Jim Jacobs recalled that the incident occurred just as the prisoners were lined up for evening *tenko*:

> We were waiting for the Japs to come and count us, when we heard the sound of planes. All heads turned towards the west, from whence the whirr of engines could be plainly heard. Headed in our direction, and coming out of the setting sun, we counted twenty-one large bombers flying at about five thousand feet. Somebody said, 'It's alright, they're Nips.' 'Like hell they are,' cried another, 'the Nips haven't any four-engine bombers.'

The raid caused extensive damage to the camp, but not to the two bridges; furthermore, 18 POWs were killed, and many more wounded. However, what was arguably worse for the POWs was the suspicion that the Allied (British and Canadian) bombers would not relent. The bridges were too strategically important. After all, if they could be disabled or destroyed, the ability of the Japanese to move men and material on the Burma–Thailand Railway would be hugely impaired.

Their suspicions were soon confirmed. With Don now living in Tamarkan, two further bombing raids targeting the bridges occurred on 8 and 13 December 1944. The second run did knock out several spans of the wooden bridge and caused slight damage to the steel bridge. Once again, though, the bombers did more damage to the camp than to the bridges, with several structures set on fire. Thankfully, this time there was no loss of life among the prisoners. In the aftermath of the bombings, Don and his mates were put to work repairing the bridges.

Work on the construction of both bridges had begun in October 1942. The wooden bridge, always intended to be a temporary structure, was completed in February 1943, while the concrete and steel bridge was finished in May 1943. Both were about 250 metres long. Trains began crossing each structure as soon as they were completed, to provide supplies to the jungle camps on the Khwae Noi.

All the POWs doing the slave labour involved in the building of the bridges were based in the Tamarkan camp, on the east side of the river, under the strict command of Lieutenant Colonel Philip Toosey. His senior medical officer was Dr Jim Mark, from Northern Ireland – the father of my friend Patricia Mark from Nanaimo.

The conditions for the POWs who had built these bridges were somewhat different from the conditions in the jungle camps, even if at first the camps were alike. Upon construction, it had five of the familiar long bamboo and attap huts, each holding 300 British and Australian men. While there was a bamboo perimeter fence, this was never intended to contain the prisoners or prevent trade with Kanchanaburi merchants, including Boon Pong. By January 1943, however, the camp was further developed. Five more huts were added to accommodate about 1,000 Dutch troops, space was created for a soccer field, and a theatre was even built for entertainment – with materials obtained from a nearby dilapidated cowshed.

During the eight months of bridge construction, conditions for the prisoners were severe, but never as horrendous as in the jungle camps. After its construction, Jim Mark was able to record with justifiable pride

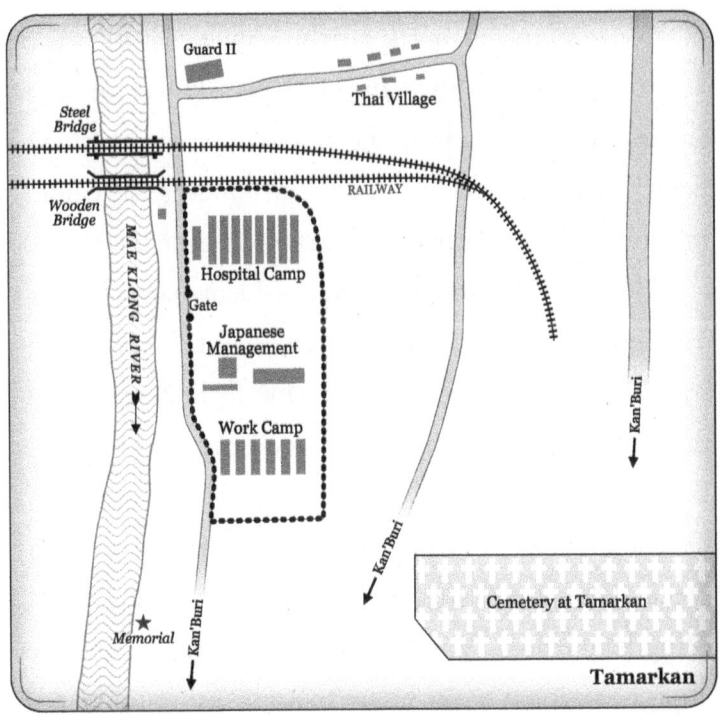

that only nine men out of 2,600 had died – a death rate of less than 0.4 per cent. This figure would have been unimaginable to the doctors in the camps further north, where death rates were 10 to 50 times higher.

Why such a difference? The most important factor was that the camp had a supply of clean water from a spring. In addition, while the quantity of food provided was the same as upriver, the quality may have been slightly better due to its proximity to established towns and roads. It was also possible to obtain supplementary food for the sick from merchants in nearby Kanchanaburi, while Tamarkan was the first camp to regularly receive food and medical supplies from the 'V' organisation and Boon Pong. There was also less jungle surrounding the camp, meaning the incidence of malaria was a little lower.

However, the determination of Lieutenant Colonel Toosey to maintain a strict regime, and thereby high morale among the men, was also critically important. The men were expected to maintain good personal hygiene. Beards were not allowed as they might harbour lice. Deep latrines were dug, with wooden covers to contain flies and maggots. Refuse was carefully disposed of, often being incinerated. Malarial drains were dug to prevent pools of stagnant water where mosquitoes would breed. The bamboo slats the men slept on were regularly drawn through fire to kill bed bugs. Toosey did a camp inspection once a week, all to avoid unnecessary illness and death.

———

The bridge was constructed with slave labour and primitive tools, particularly on the wooden trestle bridge, which was essentially built by hand using basic tools: axes, saws, chunkels and shovels, as well as rice-sack stretchers to carry soil away. It was erected on top of a foundation of wooden piles hammered deep into the silt of the river by a primitive pile-driver. The pile-driver was a steel-capped wooden block slung from a pulley on wooden scaffolding between two barges anchored in the river. It was operated by men on each barge pulling on about 20 ropes, directed by a Japanese engineer chanting 'one, two, three, four' in Japanese in a musical tone for each pull, after which the weight came down on the wooden pile.

This went on for weeks. The work was body-breaking and soul-destroying. Lieutenant Stephen Alexander later wrote: 'the monotony of it, and the primitive nature of the tools, and the sheer numbers of men slaving away – some digging, some in long snaking queues carrying baskets of earth, some chaining sand and stones from the river bed – made for a positively biblical scene.'

Further upstream, the steel and cement bridge was built on 11 concrete piers. The work was still labour-intensive, but at least the Japanese used a dredging machine and cement-mixers. The steel girders between the piers (each spanning 20.8 metres) were imported from Java.

Toosey agreed with the Japanese commandant, Lieutenant Takasaki (nicknamed 'the Frog'), to allow Allied officers to do manual work alongside the ordinary ranks. This would speed up the completion of the project, which made Takasaki happy – although his real goal was not to please the Japanese (though some accused him of being 'Jap-happy'), but to share the work more evenly and fairly among all the prisoners.

For more than two years after its completion, this concrete bridge defied attempts by Allied air bombers to incapacitate it. As previously mentioned, minor damage was done to it and the wooden bridge on numerous occasions, but the POWs would simply complete any necessary repairs within days and the bridges would go on serving the needs of the Japanese empire.

Its useful career was finally ended, however, in June 1945 by the skill of a Canadian bombing crew. On 24 June 1945, just before dawn, a squadron of 'Liberator' B-24 bombers from 159 Squadron took off from Digri, an Allied base east of Calcutta in India. Roy Borthwick, from Vancouver, was the pilot of the second-last plane to take off. He was on his final flying mission of the war. The airmen knew they had a long flight ahead of them, a 3,200km round trip, which would take 12 to 14 hours, across the Indian Ocean to the Burma–Thailand Railway. Their goal was to destroy 'Bridge 277' – the cement bridge at Tamarkan.

Borthwick's plane carried five 1,000lb (453kg) bombs. To attack the bridges he would have to descend to about 200 feet (60 metres) above the river, making five passes of the bridge and releasing one bomb with each pass. This left the huge bomber vulnerable to machine gun fire. However, Borthwick had his own technique to avoid this. He told the *Hamilton Spectator* in an interview in 1998: 'Instead of climbing up and away from the bridge after the bomb had gone, I would dive down and hug the ground, about 30 feet or so, have my nose gunner hose the area right in front of us for maybe three or four minutes, then climb up to 1,000 feet and come down again.'

His technique worked. Each of the bombs smacked into the river Mae Klong and exploded 11 seconds later. One – most likely the first – succeeded in destroying a large span of the concrete bridge. In fact, the damage was so extensive that it could not be repaired during the remaining months of the war.

Borthwick was later awarded the DFC (Distinguished Flying Cross) for his 'cool judgement, courage and great devotion to duty'. He modestly attributed his success to his bomb-aimer: 'the best in the squadron. He had a bet with his squadron boss that we would get both bridges. We got the first and just missed the second. It was my last trip and it was a good finale. This was a real stopper.'

It was indeed. This was the real end of the 'Bridge on the River Kwai'. However, Hollywood was to tell a much different story.

———

The film *The Bridge on the River Kwai* – based loosely on a novel of the same name written by a Frenchman, Pierre Boule – was released in late 1957 and was a huge box-office hit. It won seven Oscars at the 1958 Academy Awards, including best film, best director for David Lean and best actor for Alec Guinness, who played the camp commandant, Colonel Nicholson. The film and the book were, of course, works of fiction, but many who watched it mistakenly thought that it was historically accurate.

In the movie, the Japanese are shown as trying to build an inferior wooden bridge at the wrong crossing location on the river. Colonel Nicholson, to demonstrate British superiority and maintain morale, arranges for British engineers to relocate, design and build a better bridge to meet the Japanese deadline. He encourages the men to work hard for the Japanese, discourages any attempt at sabotage or escape, and is proud when they complete the work on time. One American POW, played by William Holden, does manage to escape, however. Ultimately, he becomes a member of a commando team sent back to destroy the bridge, as it is too far for the bombers to reach. At the climax of the film, a deranged Nicholson tries to prevent the saboteurs from completing their mission but is shot by one of them and falls on the detonator plunger as he dies. This blows up the bridge, sending a train carrying Japanese leaders into the river below.

Not only did the story infuriate the surviving POWs, Japanese engineers were also unhappy. One of them, Kazuyo Tsukamoto, wrote: 'We were defeated for the first time in a war, but we did not come off second-best in engineering, so, categorically, we did NOT submit to the prisoners of war who constructed the bridge.'

The POWs were upset given that the real 'Colonel of Tamarkan', the highly respected Philip Toosey, was quite unlike the fictitious Colonel Nicholson. For one thing, he encouraged his men in their efforts to sabotage the construction of both bridges. They introduced huge amounts of white ants into the wood used for the wooden bridge, for example, and tried to ensure that the cement used for the concrete bridge was mixed poorly. In January 1943, when six men tried to escape (they were soon captured, tortured and executed – two were bayoneted to death), Toosey covered up their escape for three full days. He told the Japanese that he alone knew about the escape plan, to save others from reprisals. For punishment, he was forced to stand at attention for a full day in the blistering tropical sun in full view of his men: a public humiliation. Many other beatings occurred when he stood up to the Japanese leaders on behalf of his men. Nicholson, he was not.

For Don and others, the more general historical inaccuracies in the movie were of greater concern, like how the Hollywood treatment of the railway construction lent the story an aura of glamour. He knew that the conditions he had endured were tawdry, cruel and inhumane – in fact, anything but glamorous.

———

In the real Tamarkan camp, in December 1944, Don and his mates were facing their third Christmas in captivity. He prayed that this would be his last, and that he could survive to be reunited with Nora and his family in Ireland.

The continued Allied bombing raids finally persuaded the Japanese that the camp location was too close to the bridges and too dangerous to remain occupied – especially for themselves. The commandant, Colonel Ishii, announced a plan in mid-December to move everyone across the river to the Chungkai camp, which was several kilometres away and less likely to be bombed. Ishii and his staff were the first to go, soon followed by the Allied commanding officer – an Australian, Colonel Ramsay – with some of his officers. (Colonel Toosey had been transferred to Nong Pladuk in December 1943.) Korean guards were left behind. Among the POW ordinary ranks, it was decided that the most recent arrivals, such as Don, would be the last to move. He would therefore spend Christmas at Tamarkan.

The highlight of Christmas 1944 was to be a pantomime production: 'Aladdin and his Wonderful Lamp'. There were two performances, one in the late morning and another in the late afternoon, on the stage of the Tamarkan theatre. It featured many pantomime traditions, with saucy humour, a guest appearance by Father Christmas, as well as the throwing of cigars to the audience. A beautiful 'princess' was played by a young Dutch Eurasian male prisoner, while the lead part of Aladdin was played by Ted Weller, a British prisoner with a beautiful tenor voice.

The finale of the show featured Weller singing a popular song of the time, 'The Bluebird of Happiness'. Weller inserted a variation in the second last line that stirred the emotions of all:

'Keep alive, we'll be home in '45!

Somewhere there's a bluebird of happiness.'

One of the POWs, Leslie Hall, recalled that, with this, 'the men – even those amputees who could – rose to their feet to give this song a special ovation. Tears flowed copiously, and the only dry eyes to be found were among the uncomprehending guards.'

No doubt my dad was one of those men in tears but determined to 'keep alive' and return home.

Another prisoner, John Sharp, gave a succinct summary of that Christmas Day in his secret diary: 'Performances of Aladdin given in the morning and afternoon – bright dialogue and good effects; also band concerts, a football match (British beat Dutch 3–1), boxing display etc. Informal concerts in the evening, and lights out at 11.'

After these celebrations, more and more of the POWs were moved to Chungkai or back to their previous base camps. For Don, though, there was little or no change in his daily life with the arrival of 1945. The dull, seemingly endless wait for deliverance continued.

It was, however, more obvious than ever that the war was now going against the Japanese. In a display of their growing desperation and paranoia, the Japanese leadership became fearful that the Allied officers might lead an uprising against the relatively small number of Korean and Japanese soldiers guarding the camps. To prevent this, in early February all officers in the Death Railway camps were separated from the other ranks and sent to a camp at Kanchanaburi. This meant that men like Don Kennedy would be led by NCOs or left to their own devices. A perceived consequence of this was that they would be at more risk of being slapped or beaten by the guards. Surprisingly, there was no significant increase in the number of beatings; if anything, the men felt that some of the guards were better behaved, perhaps because they feared reprisals at the end of the war. Others seemed moodier and more anxious.

On Valentine's Day, 1945 – not a day for romance this year – Don finally received confirmation of his next move. He was going back to Tamuang.

———

On 15 February 1945, Don and a few of his comrades marched southward back to Tamuang. He was pleased to discover that his old friend Dr Pavillard was still there, but he soon learned that, as at Tamarkan, no other officers were present. An NCO, Warrant Officer Christopher, was now acting as the Allied commandant in the camp. To Don's relief, there were some other ranks of 'D' Battalion still in the camp, Pavillard noting that these men had become well known for their unfailing tact and good judgement. I'm sure Don exhibited these traits in abundance, too.

The physical demands on the prisoners were minimal. There was, however, an overall increase in tension. Machine-guns were now mounted at the perimeter of the camp, facing inwards. There was also a watchtower, permanently manned by a sentry, which looked out for raids by Allied bombers. While sightings of bombers did become more frequent, they tended to be planes that had just completed an attack on the Tamarkan bridge or were en route to Bangkok. The sentry did not know this, of course, so each time he would scramble down the wooden steps of the tower, screaming, '*Hikouki, hikouki, kushu, kushu!*' ('Aeroplanes, Aeroplanes, air strike, air strike!'), and take shelter in a trench or behind a tree.

The Allied pilots did occasionally drop leaflets for the prisoners, which cheered them up. One leaflet had an unintended consequence, however. It showed the extent of Allied advances on a map of Europe and stated: 'It's in the bag, chums!' Unfortunately, the ever more nervous Japanese took this message literally and so feared that guns and ammunition were being smuggled into the camp in the rice bags. This led to every arriving rice sack being emptied out and inspected in the guard room. While this provided comic relief, it was another illustration of the strain affecting both the POWs and their captors.

The prisoners did not need these leaflets to know about the progress of the war, as the wireless set in Tamuang was still operational. They knew that Germany was close to defeat, with their armies retreating rapidly in the west before the American, British and Canadian forces, as well as giving up huge amounts of territory in the east before the rampant Russian army. As for the once-mighty Japanese, they continued a slow retreat in Burma, while American forces were in the process of taking back the Philippines.

The American Air Force, under the leadership of General Curtis LeMay, also changed bombing tactics in February 1945. Instead of attempting precision high-level daytime strikes on Japan, LeMay ordered low-level incendiary bombing at night. On 9 March 1945, 325 bombers attacked Tokyo, its wood-and-paper buildings burning easily and quickly. By the next morning, 16 square miles in the city centre had been destroyed, and 267,000 buildings burned to the ground. The heat amidst the firestorm is said to have caused the water in the city's canals to boil. Eighty-nine thousand people were killed. Many more were injured and made homeless. Still the Japanese government refused to consider surrender.

The Japanese military leadership in Thailand seemed equally determined to fight on. Every day the prisoners saw soldiers heading north on the train to Burma, with ever larger numbers of wounded and sick soldiers returning south to the Japanese hospital in Tamuang. It seemed obvious that, if and when the Japanese were defeated in Burma, the battlefield would move to Thailand. What would happen to the POWs in this scenario? Their captors would obviously not want the soldiers in Tamuang and other River Kwai base camps, or their officers in the Kanchanaburi camp, to join the ranks of an invading army. Rumours swirled among the men, but nobody had any real information.

Don undoubtedly felt the mental stress as much as his fellow POWs. However, physically, he was doing better. He had little work to do, there was a barely adequate supply of food, and Boon Pong and the 'V' organisation were still supplying extra cash and supplements. As a result, his weight and strength were finally starting to improve.

However, this improvement had an unfortunate result. In early April 1945, it was announced that a work party of 450 men would be leaving Tamuang to prepare the development of a new camp situated north-east of Bangkok. Don Kennedy's name was on the list of prisoners for the work party.

Their destination was a place called Nakhon Nayok. As they had done three years before in Singapore, the Japanese tried to convince the POWs that this move was intended to give them more room and better facilities. However, friendly Korean guards told them otherwise. They said it was a 'bumping off camp'.

They warned that no prisoners would leave that camp alive.

16 GOODBYE TO THE KWAI

NAKHON NAYOK, APRIL–JULY 1945

On 8 April 1945, Don and a few hundred other supposedly 'fit' men stood beside their kit on the parade ground of the Tamuang camp. Despite the blazing tropical sun, the men were not allowed to move or even visit the latrines. There was a general mood of apprehension. This would be a major change in the prisoners' lives, and no one really knew what lay ahead. They had no Allied officer in charge but were led by an NCO, RSM Stimson. The Japanese methodically searched each man's meagre possessions and the huts they had vacated in another search for the secret wireless set. They never found it.

Eventually, the men were marched off to the station at Tamuang to await the arrival of the southbound train.

Before they could depart, numerous wounded Japanese soldiers had to be helped from the train by the prisoners; again, the soldiers seemed scared by the sight of Europeans. Finally, the POWs were loaded into cattle trucks and the train departed. It took about two hours for the train to proceed to the 0km mark of the Death Railway at Nong Pladuk. Upon arrival, the guards took them to some filthy, dilapidated huts where the hungry prisoners spent an uncomfortable night.

The next morning, Don and his mates were given a cup of boiled rice before being marched back to the Nong Pladuk station. They sat or stood for hours in the heat, waiting for an engine to arrive to pull their train to Bangkok. (The precious wood-burning engines were hidden away in sidings at night, so that they would not be damaged by Allied bombing.) Eventually, they were loaded into the now-familiar cattle trucks, and away they went. Don was finally leaving the Burma–Thailand Railway and the River Kwai.

Progress, as usual, was slow. This time the train came to a halt at another small town, Nakhon Chai. The prisoners were pleased to discover that a bridge crossing the river at this point, the Tha Chin, had been destroyed by Allied bombing. Their mood changed, however, when they were ushered out of the cattle trucks, which were locked up by the guards, and they were told that they would be sleeping in the open. The men crawled underneath the train, many trying to find comfort by resting their heads on one sleeper and backsides on another. Bitten by swarms of hungry mosquitoes, many came down with malaria over the next two weeks.

After a wretched night, the hungry, thirsty POWs were shipped across the river in barges. They were now allowed a fire to boil the muddy river water, which they filtered through dirty pieces of cloth, each man receiving a half-pint to alleviate his thirst. Later, the Japanese provided a cup of rice. In the afternoon, a train arrived to bring them to Bangkok. This was another three-hour trip. Their entire journey, which took me less than two hours to cover by road in 2007, had taken them three days to complete.

The prisoners had not seen a major city in over three years. They were astounded by the extensive destruction of the Bangkok station and the surrounding areas, caused by Allied bombing. They were also worried for their own safety, as the station contained lots of war material such as undetonated bombs and ammunition. Having survived the deprivations of the Death Railway, it was almost unthinkable that they could now be killed by an Allied attack.

After a few hours in the station, the POWs were marched away and loaded on to some barges that already carried supplies such as rice, gasoline and ammunition. They were brought to the docks area, this again showing evidence of heavy bombardment. They unloaded the contents of the barges into some 'go-downs' (disorganised warehouses) before finally being allowed to get some sleep on the concrete floors.

The next day, the prisoners received decent food with meals of meat and vegetable stew along with some rice. They again had to work, of course, stacking bombs and ammunition to help the Japanese defend Bangkok. All the while, mental tension levels remained high, with the constant fear of an airborne attack.

On 12 April 1945, Don and his work party returned to Bangkok station and were again put to work loading war material onto a train. Once finished, they were ordered to pile into the loaded trucks and again left the war-torn city – heading north-east, for Nakhon Nayok. Throughout the 100km train journey they were sitting on or alongside the ammunition.

When the men arrived at the station, they were dismayed to learn that a 40km march still lay ahead of them. This was reminiscent of the march to the River Kwai in 1942. Each hour consisted of 50 minutes of marching, followed by 10 minutes of rest. Pressure from the guards was relentless. Men who were not keeping up were kicked, beaten with rifle butts or prodded with bayonet points. Most of this march was on a road surface, but the last few kilometres were through a rough jungle track.

Eventually, they reached their destination: an area of paddy fields and jungle at the base of a large range of hills, well away from any local village. For Don, this was Wampo all over again.

The work party was promptly put to work by the Japanese. As on the River Kwai, the initial work involved cutting down and clearing bamboo to build huts and cookhouses for themselves but also to accommodate new prisoners and guards as they arrived. Roads also had to be cleared, and latrines dug.

New parties of about 400 men arrived every week or two. Eventually, the camp held about 2,000 British, Australian and a few American POWs. The work was physically demanding and the food inadequate. Each man received about one-eighth of a pint of stew and a pint of rice three times a day. Considering the calories they were expending, this was not nearly sufficient, particularly when there were no supplements available from Boon Pong or the 'V' organisation. As a result, everyone lost weight again and vitamin deficiency diseases began to reappear. Soon one of the newly built huts had to be designated as a hospital hut. The nightmare had begun again.

Conditions became even worse when the monsoon rains began in June. The ground turned into a sea of mud, with many fields and camp areas flooding. Sometimes sewage would flow through the camp. Their captors did not care about sanitation; they relentlessly pushed the prisoners to keep digging. Soaked to the skin and exhausted, the POWs created trenches and tunnels extending into the large range of hills encircling the camp. The aim was to store supplies and petrol drums there, for the use of the Imperial Japanese Army when the Allies' anticipated attack on Thailand occurred. Given that the camp was situated in the middle of a major Japanese line of defence, the hills would give them a natural advantage. Behind this line, they had congregated about 30,000 fighting troops, who had been moved from China. These men were prepared to fight to the death to defend the emperor and the homeland.

In early July 1945, a new Allied commander arrived at the camp with a group of officers from Kanchanaburi. This was Lieutenant Colonel Philip Toosey, the 'Colonel of Tamarkan'. He had never lived in one of the jungle

River Kwai camps, so was appalled by the conditions at Nakhon Nayok. The Japanese ignored his protests, immediately forcing him and his fellow officers into strenuous manual labour. Within two weeks, Toosey – who had been healthy throughout his time in captivity – became deathly ill with bilateral pneumonia and was placed in the 'hospital' hut with about 50 other very sick men. Fortunately, the doctors by this time had a small supply of sulfonamide antibiotics, namely M&B 693 tablets. They gave him these, and he made a slow recovery.

As previously mentioned, Nakhon Nayok was many kilometres away from the nearest Thai village and had no secret radio, so Don had not heard any updates on the progress of the war since he left Tamuang. But Toosey's officers had good news. The war in Europe was over – Germany had surrendered unconditionally on 8 May 1945. Hitler was dead. They also knew that Rangoon had been recaptured by Allied forces.

Yet there was no time, or inclination, to celebrate. At the end of July 1945, in addition to the incessant rain and hard labour, there was tremendous nervous tension. The Japanese leaders were aware of the worsening war situation and that an Allied invasion of Thailand was imminent. They expected this to happen on 21 August

1945. (In fact, the Allies were planning to land in Thailand on 18 August 1945.) The Korean guards also knew that their lives were expendable as far as the Japanese were concerned, and so were clearly moody and agitated. As for the POWs, while they hoped for emancipation, rumours were rife that they would be slaughtered in the event of a Japanese retreat. All this meant that they might have only weeks to live.

Stephen Alexander, one of Toosey's trusted lieutenants, gave a succinct description of the Nakhon Nayok camp at that time: 'in squalor and working conditions it was like going back to square one on the railway in the worst days of 1943, yet just around the corner was the road to freedom – or, of course, extermination.'

Certainly Don, like the rest of his fellow prisoners, would have been praying for deliverance.

17 A NARROW ESCAPE

NAKHON NAYOK, AUGUST 1945

At the beginning of August 1945, Don was in poor condition physically, emotionally and mentally. He had lost all the weight he had regained while in Tamuang and Tamarkan. Work conditions were appalling – he was now digging through mud to build elaborate defences for his Japanese masters over an 11-hour workday – all the while living and sleeping in a wet, filthy hut miles away from civilisation of any kind.

Everyone knew that an Allied attack would happen soon. He had been a prisoner of war for almost three and a half years, surviving unimaginable challenges. With liberty possibly so close, it was agonising to think that he might be killed at this late stage. Could the rumours of imminent death at the hands of his Japanese captors really be true?

A massacre of American POWs had occurred on the island of Palawan in the Philippines in December 1944. When the Japanese mistakenly thought that Allied forces were about to land, 150 prisoners had been herded into air-raid trenches, doused in petrol and set on fire. Many who tried to escape were machine-gunned. Others climbed over a nearby cliff, but most were hunted down and bayoneted to death. Only 11 men escaped; 139 died.

The men of Nakhon Nayok did not know about this massacre, but they soon received some other troubling information. A friendly Korean guard named Haria or Haraya approached a British interpreter with alarming news. He had seen a written order to the local Japanese commander to shoot all the prisoners, and the Koreans, in the event of an Allied attack. This would be done by machine-gun. It seems the captors feared that the fitter POWs would fight with the Allied forces to overcome them. If not, the Japanese still felt that the POWs would slow them down on a retreat, as well as using up precious food supplies that they would prefer to have for themselves. The interpreter passed on the information to Lieutenant Colonel Toosey.

This written order was never found after the war. This is not unexpected, given that the Japanese tried hard to destroy any incriminating evidence. However, one such order has survived. It was written to the Japanese commandant of the Taihoku POW camp in Taiwan, to prepare for the 'final disposition' of the prisoners in the event of an attack or uprising. It is dated 1 August 1944, a year before the alleged planned events at Nakhon Nayok.

Multiple methods could be used, according to the recovered order: 'Whether they are destroyed individually or in groups, or however it is done, with mass bombing, poisonous smoke, poisons, drowning, decapitation, or what, dispose of them as the situation dictates. In any case, it is the aim not to allow the escape of a single one, to annihilate them all, and not to leave any traces.'

Toosey believed his informant and was determined that he and his men would not go down without a fight. Captain Stanley Gimson outlined his plan:

Toosey arranged that on the order being given for the massacre, Haria should bring all the Koreans with all the weapons in the guard-hut (probably only about twelve rifles and one or two light automatics) to a rendezvous. There, selected POW marksmen would take over the weapons and do what they could to hold off the attack while the rest tried to disperse into the nearby jungle. Each of us was ordered to prepare a sharpened bamboo spear to be hidden in the thatch above our bed space. At some stage it became known that two Japanese machine-gun companies were stationed near the camp to carry out the massacre. The weapons in our camp would have been of little use against them.

Ultimately, my father's life would not be saved by primitive spears, but by a new, terrible weapon that none of the soldiers had ever heard of – the nuclear bomb.

———

At the end of the Potsdam Conference in late July 1945, US President Harry Truman, after meeting with Churchill and Stalin, made a fateful decision: he would use the newly created nuclear bomb against Japan. He hoped that this would force the Japanese to surrender and therefore avoid the need for further land invasions in Asia, especially of the Japanese home islands.

On 6 August 1945, a B-29 bomber named the *Enola Gay* left Tinian in the Marianas islands bound for Japan. Over the city of Hiroshima, the American flyers dropped a uranium-based atomic bomb, nicknamed 'Little Boy'. Much of the city was instantly vaporised, and an estimated 140,000 inhabitants were killed, either immediately or in the next few weeks and months. Many more died later from the delayed effects of radiation. Most were civilians.

Truman issued a statement in the aftermath of the bombing: 'The force from which the sun draws its power has been loosed upon those who brought war to the Far East. If they do not now accept our terms they may expect a rain of ruin from the air, the like of which has never been seen on this earth.'

In fact, contrary to Truman's threat, the United States at that time had only two atomic bombs. Still, the Japanese did not know this. Neither did they reply to Truman's statement. The war went on.

On 9 August 1945, a second plutonium bomb, 'Fat Man', was dropped on Nagasaki. Estimated deaths were about 70,000. On the same day, massive numbers of Russian forces attacked the Japanese in Manchuria. Still, the Japanese War Council was equally split between those seeking peace and those who wanted to continue the war. Emperor Hirohito ultimately had to intervene, forcing a decision in favour of surrender on the morning of 10 August 1945.

Still, some military leaders would not accept the decision and fighting continued for a number of days. Finally, on 15 August 1945, at noon Tokyo time, Hirohito spoke to his subjects on the Japanese radio network. He said that the war situation had evolved 'not necessarily to Japan's advantage'. A 'new, most cruel bomb' had been used against them. As a result of this, he explained, he had ordered his government to accept Allied peace proposals.

Japan had officially surrendered.

The POWs in Nakhon Nayok were unaware of these developments and continued to fear for their lives. Rumours spread that the war was over, but nothing was confirmed. On Thursday 16 August 1945, the Japanese commander, Captain Noguchi, punished three men for minor indiscretions by forcing them to stand in front of the guardroom without food or water, all the while announcing that the war would be over by Christmas – when Britain would surrender.

Noguchi must have known about the emperor's order but did not reveal it. What he did not know was that two days earlier, the British had smuggled a radio into the camp – hidden in Noguchi's personal belongings of all places. One of the prisoners had been employed as Noguchi's personal batman, meaning he was responsible for packing and unpacking the commander's clothing at either end of his trip from Kanchanaburi. At the risk of certain execution, the batman had hidden the radio in Noguchi's suitcase on their latest trip.

For the POWs, one other problem remained after they gained possession of the radio. They had no batteries for it. Eventually, desperate for news, close to midnight on 16 August, the operators stole the battery from Noguchi's car. Once the radio was turned on, they heard a snippet of news stating that 'General MacArthur has flown to Tokyo to take control.'

Surely this meant peace? Yet Toosey was afraid to tell the men, for fear of a violent reaction from the Japanese.

Next morning, Don and his mates were sent to work as usual. Meanwhile, Noguchi left the camp for Bangkok – the car battery had been furtively returned – and Lieutenant Takasaki ('The Frog', from Tamarkan) was placed in charge.

At 5 p.m. on Friday 17 August 1945, Takasaki sent for Toosey and told him that the war was over. They were now friends, he suggested, and should therefore take tea together. However, Toosey remembered Takasaki's execution of the escapees in Tamarkan and refused the tea. Instead, Toosey gathered all the prisoners and announced that the war was over.

The initial reaction was strangely subdued. They sang the British, Dutch and American national anthems and said a prayer of thanks. They were probably too exhausted to celebrate wildly.

One of them, Lieutenant Louis Baume, summarised their feelings well. He wrote in his diary:

We have vainly hoped, prayed, planned for this day for how long – and now it has come, suddenly, unexpectedly, quietly, just like this. I suppose we ought to sing, to dance, to go mad and scream with joy but we cannot. The going has been too hard and anyway, the magnitude of the event is so great that it is quite beyond us to fully appreciate it.

A month later, Baume learned more about how near they had all come to disaster when he spoke to an Australian, Major Evitt:

He also confirms that Nakhon Nayok was to have been bombed out of existence by the R.A.F. on August 18 and that all prisoners were to have been shot by the Japanese on September 7th – the day of the invasion of Malaya and Siam. Three days, or three weeks at the most, was all we had left.

Once again, Don had narrowly escaped death. Over the next few days, he learned more about the Japanese's plan to kill the prisoners, although he probably never knew all the details I've outlined above.

However, he did know one thing for sure; finally, he was going home.

18 HOMECOMING

AUGUST–NOVEMBER 1945

'I must finish off this letter now. It's a pretty crappy sketch of three and a half years of a man's life, but someone is bound to write a book about **POW** life under the aegis of his Imp. Japanese Majesty's forces and it's going to be grim reading, so get a copy early. From what I heard in the Tokyo hospital, we Hong Kong prisoners were lucky compared to the Malayan and Philippine prisoners who were decimated by disease, starvation and brutality. The stories told by fellows who were drafted to Thailand to build a railroad through the jungle to Burma just don't seem credible. Incidentally, Don Kennedy, my Dublin pal, whom I was instrumental in sending to Malaya, was one of the unfortunates who built said railroad. I met a Singapore [sic] in Tokyo who knew Don in Thailand, and the last news he had was that Don was OK, and safely back in base camp after the railroad had been completed. I guess Don stands a good chance of being all right now. His father is Surgeon Kennedy of St. Vincent's (Butcher K.). It might also be nice to pass this on to his people.'

From *Diary of War*, by John Bernard 'Barney' Byrne. Letter written in September 1945.

In Nakhon Nayok, in the last two weeks of August, Don and his mates experienced a strange mixture of emotions. Of course there was elation, even euphoria, when they realised that their three-and-a-half-year nightmare of slavery was over. Their hearts filled with pride when they were able to raise the British, Australian and Dutch flags in the camp. Best of all, there was food. Lots of it. Herr Siegenthaler and his Swedish counterpart were determined to prevent any more deaths from starvation after the end of the war and so ensured that the POW camps throughout Thailand were supplied with food well before the official Allied relief operation got under way.

One prisoner, Major H.G. Dicker, described it: 'food was arriving by the lorry load and not a grain of rice among it – mountains of fruit, bread and freshly-roasted ducks.' The prisoners 'stuffed themselves'. To the point that medical officers became concerned, even distributing pamphlets warning about the dangers of overeating. Don, whose weight had again fallen back to six stone (84 pounds), began to gain weight for the first time since he had left Tamuang.

The joy of the POWs was tempered by the ongoing fear of the thousands of Japanese soldiers still living in the hills around the camp. These men were still armed to the teeth and had never been defeated in battle. Many Allied leaders doubted that they would ever agree to surrender. They worried that overt displays of triumph could easily trigger a massacre. As a precaution, the prisoners in Nakhon Nayok were ordered to stay in camp.

As well as fear, there was anger – particularly when the doctors in the camp discovered Red Cross medical supplies, most of them dated 1942. Those supplies would surely have saved countless Allied prisoners. Individual

Red Cross relief parcels, intended for the POWs but confiscated by the Japanese, were also found.

Allied planes began to drop leaflets in late August informing Japanese soldiers and guards that the war was really over, and that the Japanese government had surrendered. Even then, there was no certainty that this would be enough to prevent further fighting. There was only one way to find out.

On 1 September 1945, an Allied plane dropped men and supplies into Nakhon Nayok. No shots were fired. An official local surrender was acknowledged. A day later, in a ceremony in Tokyo harbour on the battleship USS *Missouri*, General MacArthur officially accepted the surrender of the Japanese nation. World War 2 was at an end.

———

Now the challenging process of getting tens of thousands of Far East POWs home could begin in earnest. Planning for this relief operation, known as Recovery of Prisoners of War and Internees (RAPWI), had been initiated months before. However, the Allied planners were somewhat unprepared for the sudden Japanese capitulation and remained rightly worried about attack by renegade Japanese soldiers until the official surrender. Further concerns included the fact that the prisoners were spread over a vast area. Many were still dangerously ill or dying, and the Allies sometimes did not even know the location of the camps, particularly those in isolated areas.

It was decided that RAPWI operations in northern parts of Asia would be controlled by the Americans, while the British would control operations in southern areas, including Thailand. Their overall commander was Lord Louis Mountbatten. He sent a notification to the Thai camps at the time of the official surrender, promising the prisoners that they would soon be going home: 'This has been a long war; but from the time you fell into enemy hands you have never been forgotten either in England or among the armies that have defeated the Japanese. I hope that it will now be only a matter of weeks before you are on your way home.'

These words would prove overly optimistic and a source of frustration for the men. Weeks later, they would nickname Mountbatten 'Linger Longer Louis'.

Back at Nakhon Nayok, Don waited patiently for the first step in the repatriation process: a move to Bangkok. The mood in the camp was now much more relaxed and joyful. He was dressed in clean shirts and shorts. Food remained plentiful, and there was an ample supply of alcohol and cigarettes provided from the closest Thai villages. Allied planes continued to drop 44-gallon drums on coloured parachutes. In addition to clothing and medicines, the drums contained soup, fruit juice, sugar, milk, coffee and cocoa, sweets and chewing gum – delightful treats that could only be dreamed about on the Death Railway.

It was now six years since the start of the war in Europe and since that beautiful summer in Ballybunion. For the first time in many years, Don could allow himself to realistically imagine a reunion with Nora. He prayed that Nora would still want him when he returned.

Around this time, the prisoners received one other pleasant surprise – a visit by Lady Edwina Mountbatten on 7 September. She gave a brief speech expressing sympathy for their plight and shook hands with each man, including Don. The visit was brief, but the boost to morale was huge.

On 10 September 1945, Don celebrated his thirty-second birthday. That day he got the best present ever: his freedom. The Allied prisoners, now stronger and better nourished, were taken by truck to the Nakhon Nayok railway station to await a train to bring them to Bangkok.

There was only one problem, and it was a big one. The train would also be used to transport many Japanese soldiers. These were not the usual Japanese or Korean guards with whom the men were familiar. These were battle-hardened soldiers, men who had not yet handed over their arms. Many showed by their surly attitude that they were still reluctant to accept surrender, a notion foreign to their *bushido* warrior code. Likewise, some of the younger ex-POWs were keen to take revenge on these hated enemies.

The soldiers from both sides were loaded into separate railroad carriages. Don, who was perhaps older and more mature than many of his headstrong younger colleagues, was ordered to guard the Japanese carriages while the train was en route to Bangkok. A nerve-wracking and seemingly endless journey ensued. Thankfully, there was no violence.

Don arrived in the capital of Thailand unharmed – and a free man.

The Allied ex-prisoners were once again accommo-dated in large warehouses at the port of Bangkok. Unlike their previous stay, this time there were no brutal Korean guards to intimidate or beat them; in fact, they were free to do as they pleased. Many wanted to make up for lost time and so lost all sense of discipline. Bangkok's bars, brothels and restaurants became busy. Jack Leeman of the War Graves Commission described the situation well:

'The ex-prisoners really let their hair down with a bang. They drank anything regardless of taste, cost or effects. The girls in the extensive red-light district were kept fully employed day and night.'

Don was still malnourished and exhausted. His health was precarious. As a result, his main focus was to get some rest and gain some weight. He also wanted to notify Nora and his family that he was still alive, and so sent them letters and telegrams. He had no idea that his mother had died in Dublin in December 1944.

Back in Ireland, my mother received a copy of a British Red Cross publication dedicated to relatives of Japanese prisoners, *The Far East*. The editorial of the September issue gave encouraging news: 'The long night is ended. The grim silence is broken. Cables are streaming into their parents and wives from prisoners and internees announcing their release after years of captivity. Soon they themselves will follow.'

Don wanted to get out of Bangkok as soon as he could. Not only had discipline deteriorated among the Allied troops, but there was also fighting between the local Thai and Chinese populations. One ex-prisoner was killed in crossfire between these two groups.

Another victim of violence was Boon Pong in Kanchanaburi. In early September 1945, he was shot by Thai police outside his shop in front of his wife and father, sustaining wounds in his neck and the back of his chest. The cause is unclear, but it may have been a case of mistaken retribution. It seemed likely that he would die, but a British officer, Captain Newell, bundled him and his wife into Newell's car and drove him to the hospital hut at Tamuang. Here a medical team gave him blood transfusions, as well as a new antibiotic called penicillin, and operated on his wounds. He made a full recovery. He was awarded the King's Medal for Courage in the Cause of Freedom by the British government after the war. He was also honoured by the Dutch government, being named an officer of the Order of Orange-Nassau.

In Bangkok, some were frustrated at what they felt was the slow progress of evacuation. They joked that RAPWI really stood for 'Retention of All Prisoners of War Indefinitely'. In reality, the process was progressing as efficiently as it could under such difficult circumstances.

In late September 1945, to his relief, Don began the next stage of his journey home. He was driven by truck to Bangkok's Don Mueang Airport, which was a hive of activity. Large planes circled continuously overhead, awaiting their turn to land. After they had discharged cargoes of supplies and armed soldiers, he eventually got to board one of these planes, on which he and a couple of dozen other ex-prisoners were flown to Rangoon.

Somehow, as the plane took off, Ireland seemed a lot closer.

———

After the chaos of Bangkok, Rangoon was a pleasant surprise. As soon as they landed, the men were met by nurses and given a brief medical inspection. After the inspection, they entered tents or canteens which contained tables with white tablecloths, endless plates of sandwiches and real tea. Stanley Pavillard found the experience emotional: 'we were taken to a WVS [Women's Voluntary Service] canteen, where charming girls came up and made much of us; we were not used to this, and found ourselves inexplicably liable to hysterical tears.'

Later, they were brought to hospitals in the Rangoon area, where they were assessed for infections or any medical treatments they might need. Some of the men from the River Kwai camps, perhaps including my father, made little of their disabilities for fear that their return home would be delayed.

Those deemed fit for onward travel – including my dad – were moved to transit camps, officially called

'Forward Area Reinforcement Holding Units', to await their voyage home. Here, they experienced another shock: real beds, with springs and mattresses and crisp white sheets. It was another taste of home comforts.

They continued to eat copiously, gaining weight and strength. They were provided with more new clothing. Red Cross welfare officers, both male and female, were attentive and even arranged entertainment. This included sightseeing trips, as well as shopping excursions and bathing. Cables and letters home were also sent by all.

To her absolute delight and relief, Nora received her first uncensored letter from Don in three and a half years. He assured her that he still loved her, and that he still wanted to marry her. He made no mention of the horrors he had endured. She was now sure that he had survived the war. However, she had no idea how long it would take him to return to Ireland.

Back in Rangoon, Don patiently waited as the Royal Navy scrambled to provide enough ships to return the prisoners home. These recovery ships included purpose-built troopships as well as some aircraft carriers, which could accommodate large numbers of men and support staff.

After a couple of weeks, Don was notified that he would be sailing home. While there is no official record of the ship he travelled on, it may well have been the SS *Orbita*. Lieutenant Colonel Toosey, the commander in Nakhon Nayok and Tamarkan, had pulled some strings to ensure that all the men under his leadership could travel together, and so they were assigned to this 16,532-ton ship, formerly of the Pacific Steam Navigation Company. It left the port of Rangoon on Wednesday, 11 October 1945. A voyage of 8,000 miles lay ahead.

Unlike his dangerous outward-bound sailing in 1940, this time Don could travel via the Suez Canal, reducing the travel time to just over four weeks. The ships were well stocked with extra food, and there were doctors, nurses and welfare officers on board, so the men continued to recover on their way home. Don's overall weight gain was about average – two stone (28 pounds) – bringing his weight up to eight stone (112 pounds). He was still massively underweight, of course, but in much better health than before.

His ship stopped at a number of ports along the way: Colombo in Ceylon (now Sri Lanka), Port Said in Egypt and Gibraltar in the Mediterranean Sea. At each port, they received a warm welcome from the assembled ships at anchor, as well as more letters from home. Most of the letters were well received, although a few did notify soldiers that their wives or girlfriends had left them for other men during their time away. On the SS *Orbita*, they even formed a 'Jilted Lovers' Club' for these unfortunate returnees.

Don was not one of the jilted lovers. Nora's letters assured him that she had remained faithful to him, and that she still loved him. She would travel from Mallow to Dublin to greet him when he returned.

As they got closer to Britain, Don was supplied with warmer clothing; this was probably not well-fitting or flattering but was at least more suitable for the cool November weather.

Finally, after 29 days, his ship arrived in Liverpool. There were salutes and sirens from the nearby ships and most of the ex-POWs enjoyed emotional reunions with family and friends. Don had no such joy. One leg of his journey remained.

Before he could leave for Ireland, his Japanese prisoner of war form had to be recorded and processed. This record, no. 29940, would be retrieved by my sister Irene in Kew 65 years later. In it, he documented his length of stay in each camp with the name of the camp leader, and stated that he was not involved in any escapes or sabotage. I wonder how traumatic it must have been for him to fill out that document, reliving memories of the horrors he had experienced.

———

Don returned to Dublin the same way he had left it more than five years previously – via ferry across the Irish Sea. First, he took a train from Liverpool to Holyhead in north Wales, then the ferry to Dún Laoghaire.

The Ireland he was returning to, as a strictly neutral country, still referred to the war as 'The Emergency'. The country was economically depressed, and there was ongoing widespread rationing of items such as petrol, coal and many food items. News coverage of the war had been censored, and de Valera had even expressed his condolences in person at the German Embassy in Dublin on the death of Hitler. Returning British soldiers would not receive any official recognition or praise, Don would soon learn; the government attitude was one of ignorance and indifference. There would be no Irish medals or marching bands.

On a grey November day he finally arrived home. He was greeted by a group of family and friends, including his fiancée Nora, his father Denis and his old friend Jim Trainor.

He was devastated to learn that his beloved mother had died the previous December. However, there was some consolation in learning that his brothers Dick and

Dermot had survived the war. Neither of them could be present to meet him, as they were still completing their military duties.

Nora was shocked by her fiancé's appearance. His new, British government-issued suit hung loosely on his tall, thin frame. When she had last seen him, he had weighed about 12 stone (168 pounds). She thought he now looked scrawny and skeletal. His sense of humour also seemed to have disappeared.

As the days passed, she also grew upset that he was reluctant to talk about his wartime experiences. She had little or no understanding of the horrors he had experienced and worried that they could not build a life together if he could not be open and honest.

Jim Trainor had an idea to lift the mood. He insisted that he would treat them both to dinner at the famous Jammet's restaurant in Nassau Street in central Dublin. Founded in 1901 by brothers Michel and François Jammet, it soon established a worldwide reputation for haute cuisine – with correspondingly high prices. Trainor told my parents not to worry about the cost of the meal. He wanted to celebrate the survival of his best friend.

When they arrived, my usually frugal parents were astounded by the huge range of food that was available – and the cost. Don decided to order an expensive steak, something he had dreamed about in those long days by the River Kwai. When it arrived, there was only one problem: the steak was covered in onions. Lots of them. My father hated onions. What should he do? To my mother's embarrassment, and the indignation of a snooty waiter, he insisted on sending the meal back to the kitchen. A few minutes later, the plate of steak returned, minus the onions. The frostiness of the waiter seemed to wash away the tension between the couple, and my parents exploded in laughter.

Soon, with the assistance of fine food and lots of wine, they were exchanging jokes and stories like they had in Ballybunion in the summer of 1939. The old Don Kennedy was back. My mother recognised that the war had damaged his body and his spirit, but it had not succeeded in destroying them. She was confident they would have a long life together.

Their love had survived.

19 HUMAN IMPACT OF THE DEATH RAILWAY

'(They) were different men when they returned to their homes at the end of 1945. Some managed to integrate those terrible years into their lives and make it part of their whole. They were the lucky ones. But they all suffered. Alcoholism, depression, suicide, marital disaster, lingering legacies of malnutrition, infestation and disease were commonplace. The catalogue of their pain seems endless. And yet, they managed to adapt, adjust, move on.'

Dr Patricia Mark, 1995

It is impossible to quantify the massive personal costs, in terms of disability and death, to the unfortunate people forced to build the Burma–Thailand Railway. Vast numbers died during the construction period. Many more died after the railway was completed, and some died in the hospital camps even after the Japanese surrendered. As Paddy Mark mentions above, those who survived often suffered silently for the rest of their lives. Others, perhaps even my father, died premature deaths years later from the ill-effects of their imprisonment.

It's also important, when statistics are produced, to remember that each number in the calculations represents an individual, usually young and previously healthy, who became an innocent victim of the brutal, relentless Japanese war machine. Had their taskmasters adhered to the terms of the Geneva Convention, some would undoubtedly still have died. However, most would not.

The vast majority of those who died were not even soldiers. They were the native labourers, the 'romusha', or 'coolies', supposedly allies of the Japanese who had been lured to the River Kwai by false promises of well-paid work and good working conditions. They came from Malaya, Thailand, Ceylon, Java and Burma. Only rough estimates can be given for the number of deaths among these workers. Rod Beattie of the Thailand–Burma

Railway centre in Kanchanaburi estimates that 85,400 died, out of a total workforce of just over 175,000. Most of their bodies were incinerated or buried in mass graves, with no record of their locations. Even as late as November 1990, a mass grave containing about 700 bodies – probably Tamil forced labourers – was dug up about one hundred metres from Kanchanaburi Town Hall.

In contrast, the records for deaths of Allied POWs are relatively accurate and well documented. Clifford Kinvig says that a total of 61,806 men were forced to work on the Death Railway and that at least 12,399 died – over 20 per cent of the total. This contrasts with the death rate for British POWs held by Germany, which has been estimated at about 3.5 per cent. British railway deaths were 6,904, with over 2,500 deaths each for Australians and Dutch forces. The bodies of 337 US prisoners were also repatriated after the end of the war.

Most of those who died were regular soldiers, known as 'other ranks', like Don. Officers had a much lower death rate. Brian MacArthur quotes some telling statistics. Among the Australians in F Force, 1,065 other ranks died, but only three officers. In H Force, 26 officers died, a death rate of 6 per cent. However, there were 627 deaths among British other ranks (37 per cent),

165 among Australian other ranks (27 per cent) and 33 among the Dutch (7 per cent).

This was not because the officers received better food rations from the Japanese; they received the same calories as their men. In most cases, however, they did not have to do the same arduous labour as the other ranks, so they lost weight at a slower rate. They also received higher rates of pay than the regular soldiers. While much of this money was donated to canteen funds for the sick, they still had some left over to purchase food privately to supplement their rations. This understandably caused some resentment among the other ranks.

Still, some officers were highly respected because of their leadership skills and their ability to maintain morale and discipline in the camps. For example, Philip Toosey insisted that he and his fellow officers should also participate in manual work. Officers like him and Weary Dunlop were prepared to argue with the Japanese, sustaining severe beatings and torture as a result. In this way, they undoubtedly saved many lives.

In Don's case, he was fortunate to be in camps under the leadership of men like Dunlop and Toosey, as well as the medical care provided by brave medical officers such as Stanley Pavillard. Their presence may well have been the difference between life and death.

Another factor was how the war ended. The decision to drop the atom bombs on Hiroshima and Nagasaki was monumental. Critics will rightly say that the deaths of innocent civilians caused by these bombs were unimaginably cruel and numbered about 200,000. It is also true, however, that the war would have continued for months or years longer without these bombs, with a huge amount of further deaths. The Americans estimated that they would have sustained about a million casualties (dead and wounded) among their soldiers if they had been forced to invade the Japanese home islands. Many more millions of Japanese – both soldiers and civilians – would have died from military action, fire-bombing, disease and starvation.

When these matters are debated, the POWs held by the Japanese are often forgotten. I think it's clear that over 100,000 of these men would have been ruthlessly executed if conventional war had continued. Pavillard sums it up well: 'The world has talked about nuclear weapons at great length since August 1945; but I cannot get it out of my head that if it had not been for these weapons we would all have died.'

20 MARRIED LIFE

My parents married on 24 April 1946 in St Patrick's Church in Cork. They had been engaged for six years. The best man was Jim Trainor and the bridesmaid was my mother's only sister, Kathleen Ring. My paternal grandfather, Denis Kennedy, and maternal grandmother, Mary Ring, were guests of honour.

By this time, Don had gained back more weight, now weighing a little over 10 stone (140 pounds). But rationing was still the norm in Ireland. The hotel in Cork where the wedding reception was held could not even sell alcohol, so it had to be brought from Mallow, where my mother was living. At the end of the celebration, one of the attendees volunteered to bring the leftover booze back to Mallow – unsurprisingly, it never arrived.

Don and Nora on their wedding day, 24 April 1946

One family member who could not make the wedding was Don's brother Dick. In February 1946, because he could speak German, he was assigned to Germany as chaplain to the College of the Rhine Army in Göttingen. After about fifteen months there, Dick returned to his previous role as a Jesuit priest and teacher in Wah Yan College, Kowloon, Hong Kong and, for a time, in Canton, China.

In Canton, after the Communist take-over, he got into trouble with the authorities in 1953 for continuing his Catholic missionary work, and spent over a month in prison. He was expelled and returned to his teaching career in Hong Kong, which he loved. Like Don, he rarely spoke about his experiences as a Japanese POW, but he did write a memoir of his imprisonment in China. His *Canton Chronicle* is one of my most treasured possessions. In the mid-1980s, doctors in Dublin told him he had terminal cancer, and advised him to stay in Ireland. However, he insisted that Hong Kong was his home, and he returned there, continuing to work until shortly before he passed away on 22 August 1986.

After the wedding, Don continued his search for work. The Irish economy was still stagnant, so employment opportunities were limited. However, he was highly regarded professionally in Malaya and so was soon offered a position in an accountancy firm in Kuala Lumpur. This he accepted, and the newly-weds booked passage to sail to Malaya at the end of June.

In the interim, Don's sister Una and her husband, Seamus Rourke, kindly gave them the use of their house in Mount Merrion Avenue in Dublin. For the first time, my mother witnessed the nightmares and sweats that tormented Don each night. His wartime trauma had left its mark, she realised, and would not be easily overcome.

After another ferry trip from Dublin to Holyhead, they set sail from Liverpool bound for Singapore on 25 June 1946, on board the Cunard ship *Mauretania*. There were almost 700 passengers on board, but conditions were far superior to Don's previous voyages in 1942 and 1945, not least because they were able to sail through the Suez Canal and there was no food rationing. Nora was perhaps less interested in this than Don, being preoccupied with another issue – she was already pregnant with their first child.

———

They arrived in Singapore in late July 1946 before travelling to Kuala Lumpur, where they set up home at 633 Circular Road. They settled in well to life in the city.

They made friends among the expat community. Nora was able to resume playing hockey, a popular (and multi-racial) sport in Malaya. They both played golf.

Then Don received a letter from Ireland. It was from his father, telling him that he had decided to remarry. He needed someone to look after him as he got older, he explained. His new fiancée, Bridget Troy, was one of his operating room nurses and was less than half his age – he was 77, she was 38. This news was too much for Don; he was devastated. The man who had not cried about his war experiences broke down and shed bitter tears.

Not surprisingly, Don did not return to Dublin to attend the wedding in January 1947. My parents were instead focused on a happier event – the safe arrival a month later of Mary Clare. Two years later, in August 1949, Cecily was born.

Their lives seemed comfortable. They had a wide circle of friends. Don was well paid, and my mother had paid help to assist her with child-rearing and meal preparation. They even had time to fly to Singapore, staying at the world-famous Raffles Hotel. They met some of Don's wartime friends there, including Dr Pavillard, who had most deservedly been awarded the Member of the Most Excellent Order of the British Empire (MBE) in 1947 for his wartime efforts.

Yet there were growing complications for their way of life. Asians everywhere were demanding – and soon fighting for – independence. The old colonial powers, including Britain, France and the Netherlands, no longer had the resources to enforce their rule. For example, the 'Jewel in the British Crown', India, had been granted independence in 1947.

Malaya did not obtain its independence from Britain until 1957. From 1948 on, however, the Malayan Communist Party (MCP) began armed resistance against British rule, and incidents of violence, kidnapping and killing aimed at white people became increasingly frequent. By 1950, my parents felt that the country was no longer safe for themselves and their two young daughters.

It was time to return to Ireland.

The journey home was not without incident. Cecily became very ill on the voyage. She was assessed by the ship's doctor who drunkenly told my mother to 'have a few drinks, because the child will be dead by morning'. In typical fashion, she decided to prove him wrong, keeping the 10-month-old baby alive with frequent small sips of liquid through the night. Cecily was later found to have lactose intolerance and made a full recovery.

———

Back in Ireland, they lived with my grandmother Mary Ring over her drapery shop in Mallow.

One day, Don and Nora travelled to Cork to have lunch with a special friend and his wife; this was the Irish doctor with the Red Cross who had slipped the vitamin pills to Don on the Death Railway back in 1943. The two men conversed easily, talking about many things, including their love for Ballybunion. Most importantly, of course, my parents thanked the doctor for saving my father's life.

Sadly, the name of this doctor has been lost in the sands of time. Later in her life, my mother could not remember it, and neither I nor my siblings had written it down when she was younger. His name is not recorded in the ICRC archives in Geneva, nor in the Swiss government archives. I still retain a faint hope that perhaps someday one of his descendants will read this book and reveal his identity to the Kennedy family. We certainly owe him a deep debt of gratitude for his kindness and courage.

The most pressing issue at this time for Don was to find long-term employment. The Irish economy was still sluggish, although starting to improve. In the 1950s, much of rural Ireland was still without electricity supply, which perpetuated the pattern of widespread poverty and emigration. The Irish Rural Electrification Scheme was a massive project designed to correct this. A Belgian electrical company named ACEC, which manufactured transformers and other electrical supplies needed for the scheme, decided to open a factory in Waterford on the outskirts of the city. In 1951, Don was selected to be the company secretary (perhaps now his job title would be chief operating officer) of the new factory, second in command to a Belgian CEO, M. Marchand. He had finally secured employment.

The Kennedy family, now with the addition of baby Irene, moved to Atlantic View, Tramore, a few miles from Waterford. The move went smoothly, although there was one significant problem: my mother was not a cook. In Kuala Lumpur and in Mallow, others had done this work for her. Now she was expected to feed her family.

Their next-door neighbours were Luke and Ethna O'Sullivan. Luke was also on the management team of ACEC, while Ethna was another novice cook who was expected to put nutritious food on the table for her growing family. Ethna and Nora devised a plan. Each day they would try out the same recipes on their unsuspecting husbands and families. They would then compare notes, keeping the meals which were a success and dumping the failures. Somehow, both families survived.

ACEC became a major employer in the city of Waterford, second only to the world-famous Waterford Crystal factory. The company purchased two houses on land neighbouring the factory, named Tycor House and Windhoek. In 1952, the Kennedys moved into Tycor House, while the Marchand family lived in Windhoek. Four more children arrived: Denis in 1952, myself in 1954, Valerie in 1956 and Louise in 1960. When M. Marchand died in 1963, Don became CEO and we moved a few hundred yards to Windhoek.

With seven children to raise, my parents' lives were busy. My father tried his best to help with childcare, which was not common for men in that era. On Sunday afternoons, he would often announce that we were going on a 'mystery tour', while my mother took a nap. How we all managed to fit in a medium-sized car, I do not know. We would go to see the beautiful scenery in the nearby Knockmealdown Mountains or perhaps visit one of the many beaches near Waterford. With so many children, it was almost impossible to have a summer holiday for the entire family. I can only remember doing this once, in the summer of 1959. The reader will probably not be surprised at the destination.

We went to Ballybunion.

———

In 1965, my father became a member of the board of directors of Waterford Football Club. At the end of that season, the team finished last in the League of Ireland, after which my father was chosen to be the board chairman. He set about applying his business principles to the running of the club and, within a year, they were the league champions. In his eight years as chairman, they won the league six times: in 1966, 1968, 1969, 1970, 1972 and 1973. The club has never won the league since then.

After their 1968 victory, Waterford qualified to play in the European Cup and had the good fortune to be drawn against Manchester United in the first round. United were the European champions that year and immensely popular in Ireland. They had three legendary world-class players: Bobby Charlton of England, Denis Law of Scotland and – my personal idol – George Best of Northern Ireland.

The first game of the two-legged contest was to be held in Ireland. Demand for tickets to the game was huge. Waterford's home ground could only accommodate a few thousand spectators, so everyone expected the game would be played at Dalymount Park in Dublin, as it could accommodate 40,000 people. This was where all Irish football international games were played at the time.

My father and his board had other ideas, however. He knew that, of those 40,000 people at Dalymount Park, only three to four thousand could be seated, with the rest standing on terraces. And seats were valuable, as seated tickets could be priced at about 10 times the cost of standing tickets. This brought another venue to mind: Lansdowne Road. In contrast to Dalymount, at Lansdowne Road – the home of the Irish rugby team – there was room for 50,000 spectators, with 25,000 seats. Up till then, a soccer game had never been held in the ground. However, seeing the potential windfall for his club, my father signed an agreement with the Irish Rugby Union, confirming Lansdowne Road as the venue for the game. The financial bonanza for Waterford was huge, funding their successes in the years to come.

Soon after, all the major football games, including international games, were played at Lansdowne Road (now known as the Aviva Stadium). This continues to the present day – and all because of a pioneer, Don Kennedy.

Don gave back to the Waterford community in many ways. As well as being an effective chairman of Waterford Football Club, he became a founder member of Waterford Lions in the mid-1960s, a service club which raised – and continues to raise – funds for many good local causes. To continue his legacy, my brother Denis is now an active member.

Through all this, Nora 'ran a tight ship'. Rules were followed and timelines were kept. If a child rebelled, one parent backed up the other. Corporal punishment, common at that time, was never used; perhaps Don had seen, and experienced, enough of this during the war. In return, each child was guaranteed security and stability, encouragement to follow their dreams, a good education and, most important, unconditional love.

It was a successful recipe. Our house was truly a home.

———

My parents left Windhoek in 1971 when they bought a house in South Parade in the centre of Waterford. When my father retired from ACEC in 1978, we – his now adult children – bought him a greenhouse, which was duly erected in the back garden. However, after about six months, the greenhouse was returned; he was bored. Instead, he returned to part-time work in a nearby accountancy firm for a few years, before gradually easing into retirement mode.

In the 1980s, my parents finally found time to travel to hotter climates in Europe and Florida (the home of my sister Valerie) and to socialise with friends and their ever-expanding family. Dad was involved with the Lions Club, supported Waterford FC without the stress of running it, and caught up on reading and current events. He enjoyed daily walks and keeping a small garden.

Don died in July 1989 of stomach cancer. His health had been declining for several months, but he bore his illness with typical stoicism. Less than two days before his death, he was still distributing communion at Mass.

My mother outlived him by 27 years. She travelled the world, visiting her ever-expanding family (including a trip to see us in Canada), remained busy with local charities and lived independently in her own home until October 2016, when she fell and broke her hip. Even then, she had successful surgery and was making great progress with rehabilitation when she had a massive stroke. All seven of her children were able to return to Waterford from different parts of the world to be with her and have the privilege of participating in her bedside care. She passed away four days shy of her ninety-ninth birthday.

My parents were truly a couple. In the years after my father passed, when I returned to Waterford, I often invited my mother to come with me when I visited his grave. She would always reply that she didn't need to go, as he was always with her.

11ᵗ Oct.1989.

Charter Lion, Don Kennedy, dies in Waterford.

What made this perfect specimen of 6'2" tick? - tall, lean, with perfectly coordinated movements. These physical characteristics were outshone even by his personality traits of calmness, consideration, concern for others and a beautiful sense of humour.

This was our Charter Lion - Lion Don Kennedy, who died recently, having borne his illness with the dignity and courage that were always part of his life. Most of the characteristics of this wonderful man were naturally genetically begotten and modified by his family environment but they must have been tempered by his experience in the Far East during the last war.

Don was working as a chartered accountant in Kualalumpur when the war was declared. He later volunteered for the British Army and became a prisoner of war when Singapore fell to the Japanese.

He was a prisoner in the infamous Changi and worked on the Burma Road for three and a half years. He had many harrowing experiences each day but his worst day was when he had to bury twenty-one of his own comrades in one day. He was barely six stones when freed. One does not leave experiences like that behind without its affecting one's own character.

He brought his compassion and concern everywhere with him. His strength of character was extraordinary to the end. All were demonstrated in his Lionism. He was very honoured to be a Minister of the Eucharist and actually distributed the Eucharist to his fellow parishioners thirty-six hours before he died.

Non tetigit quod non ornavit.

We are not likely to know his like again. All members of Waterford Lions Club deeply regret Don's passing and we extend to his wife, Nora and the Kennedy family our deepest sympathy.

Obituary of my father written in
October 1989 by a Waterford Lions Club member

EPILOGUE

On 6 June 2007, Maggie and I strolled across the Bridge on the River Kwai at Tamarkan as the waters of the Khwae Yai flowed gently below. The damaged bridge had been repaired soon after the end of the war, using funds and materials supplied as reparation by the Japanese government. It was one of the most emotional moments of my life. My father had walked across this bridge too, albeit under very different circumstances from mine. I wore smart new clothes and shoes and had travelled there in a comfortable air-conditioned minibus. He had probably been barefoot, wearing some filthy rags, while Japanese or Korean guards forced his exhausted, malnourished body to keep marching with screams and rifle butts. I felt tears welling up in my eyes as I walked, and an unfamiliar tightness in my chest.

It was appropriate, if completely coincidental, that it was D-Day. This was the technical term used by the Allied military planners for the seaborne invasion of Normandy in 1944, a pivotal moment in World War 2. I thought of the many pivotal moments in my father's wartime experiences which enabled him to survive. In 1943, he might have died from beriberi but for a miraculous chance meeting with an Irish Red Cross doctor. He avoided cholera amid a deadly outbreak. In 1944, he could have been chosen to travel to Japan on a hell ship and been sunk by an Allied submarine. Later that year, he could have been killed by Allied bombing near the exact spot I was standing on. In 1945, he would surely have been machine-gunned by Japanese soldiers if the war had lasted a few weeks longer.

Earlier that morning, when we arrived in Kanchanaburi, our first stop had been at the war cemetery. Here there were thousands of neat, beautifully maintained graves, lovingly tended by Thai gardeners. Each grave was identified by a simple brass plaque, with a small flowering plant alongside it. I read some of the names and dates of death as I walked the paths between the graves. The soldiers lying here had originated in the Netherlands, Australia and Britain, and the vast majority were under 25 years old when they died – young men in their prime, killed by cruelty and neglect. I imagined that few of these graves had been visited by a parent, lover or descendant. My father could so easily have been interred here, far from his home and family.

For the final part of our River Kwai pilgrimage, we were able to travel north by train over the wooden Wampo viaduct. I wondered if any of the original timbers erected by my father still survived. How many of his friends and colleagues had died here under the conditions of 'Speedo' for the benefit of the Imperial Japanese Army? The train ride finished at what is now known as Namtok. My father would have called this place Tarsau, the site of his personal miracle on the River Kwai. It seemed an appropriate place to end our journey.

I still wonder why my dad survived when so many others did not. Yes, there were the key incidents mentioned above, but surely there were other reasons. He had the good fortune to be involved with some exceptional leaders, such as Pavillard, Dunlop and Toosey, I suppose. Under trying circumstances, these officers – unlike many others – were prepared to stand up to their Japanese captors, outsmarting them whenever they could.

Likewise, he was lucky to be assigned to camps that benefited from the services of the courageous and clever Boon Pong. He too was able to frequently outwit

A train on the River Kwai, Wampo viaduct
(© Shutterstock / Kan Kankavee)

the Japanese, unafraid to put his life on the line for the benefit of the Allied POWs.

My father's personal attributes were also of major importance, I believe. He was older than the average POW and better educated. Both Pavillard and Toosey felt that this type of prisoner had a better experience of life and adversity, and was therefore more likely to follow instructions and less likely to act angrily or impulsively. He also had a strong religious faith, which never wavered despite the horrors he saw, instead helping him to endure each new challenge with quiet courage.

He had also grown up as part of a large but close-knit family of 11 children. His father was strict but fair, while his mother ensured that each of them knew that they were loved unconditionally. This family size ensured that Daddy knew how to be a team player. This – and his easy-going, sociable personality – made it easy for him to adjust as part of any large group.

I think, however, that his most important asset was the love he carried in his heart for his soulmate, my mother. When conditions were at their worst, whether physically, mentally or emotionally, this was what gave him the strength to persevere and endure. He was rewarded with 43 years of marriage to the love of his life. He surely earned that reward.

A couple of years after my visit to the River Kwai, similar thoughts and emotions affected my sister Irene when I asked her to try to obtain dad's POW records at the British National Archives in Kew. She wrote me a brief description of her visit, which I think is worth sharing:

It was an anxious journey to the National Archives in Kew – I knew it had to be done, but wasn't looking forward to finding the proof of my father's detention as a POW with the Japanese. Although we had all heard the story of Daddy's horrifying experience, it had always (as a child) seemed just that – a grim story that was only rarely and sparingly mentioned in our home.

The staff at Kew were extremely helpful, and supplied me with a bunch of files which would hopefully contain the one I needed to access – and it wasn't too long before I found the one I'd come to see. It was indeed shocking to see Daddy's name and personal details there – evidence of the dreadful and lengthy ordeal he'd been subjected to – along with so many other innocent people. Daddy had always referred to me as a 'crybaby' – and on this occasion I didn't let him down! It was the shocking reality and sheer sadness of it all – the proof in black and white that this horrific episode had actually happened – date of capture, movement from one dreadful camp to another – his life and freedom stolen, and being referred to as a number for the duration of that terrifying time?

A small crumb of comfort I found was that, unlike other names I came across in the files, Daddy seems to have mainly toed the line, and was therefore not subject to any gruesome punishments which undoubtedly came the way of other prisoners who had black marks on their files due to attempted escapes, lack of cooperation etc. I'm sure he wasn't always on his best behaviour, but at least I knew that if he had transgressed, he'd managed to get away with it!

In any case, I came away that day with copies of the records to pass on to Fergus, which was the purpose of my visit. I was (and still am) filled with gratitude that our amazing father had survived his ordeal with such courage and fortitude, and gone on to lead a full and happy life, touching the lives of so many with his quiet wisdom and strength of character.

Irene brings up another important topic, one which has always intrigued me. Our father had experienced major life-threatening trauma and seen first-hand the death of many of his colleagues from disease and malnutrition. Surely having to bury a large number of cholera victims, who were his personal friends and colleagues, must have left horrible images in his memory. Every day of captivity had been filled with anxiety, fear and uncertainty. He could have been punished, tortured or executed for any infraction, real or imagined. Mass extermination of all prisoners remained a real possibility, even after Japan's official surrender.

Despite all this, on his return to civilisation, he received no professional counselling. Only my mother was aware of the terrible nightmares. In those days, the conventional wisdom was that he should simply forget about it, get on with his life and perhaps drown out those memories in a blur of alcohol, if necessary. No one had heard of post-traumatic stress disorder, but many of the survivors from the Death Railway experienced exactly that.

On top of all this, in 1945 and again in 1950, my dad returned to a country that was poor and introspective. Ireland did not want to have an open discussion about the war and certainly had no intention of acknowledging the bravery of any Irish citizen who had been involved.

Ambivalence about the role of Irish soldiers in both World Wars continues to the present day. At least officially, no one in Ireland was going to call him a hero.

Why was he not angry, bitter or an alcoholic upon his return? It surely would have been easy for him to carry a chip on his shoulder and feel hard done by. There must have been many days when he felt down and depressed, remembering in detail the horrors of the Death Railway. Those are experiences no one can forget.

Instead, my father decided that those memories would not define him. He tapped into his reserves of courage and character and chose to focus on his community, his work, the underprivileged – and, most important, his family.

He was hardworking, intelligent and a natural leader. In his dealings with others, he was always scrupulously honest, kind and thoughtful. He was patient and level-headed and had a great sense of humour. He chose optimism over pessimism, happiness over sadness.

However, his family was always his number one priority. Though he would never show it publicly, he took great pride in his children's successes in their academic studies, sports and careers. He warmly welcomed two daughters-in-law and four sons-in-law into the family and showed his love for young grandchildren as they came into the world. He knew that he had a happy and tight-knit family. For me, he modelled how to be a husband, a father and a man.

Yet he was always humble about his achievements and never sought the limelight. Public acclaim was not his thing. This was especially true with regard to his wartime experiences. He never applied for wartime service medals and would certainly not have worn them if he had received them. He was also not interested in compensation for his mistreatment as a POW. (Ironically, in the early 2000s, years after he died, my mother did receive a compensation payment on his behalf from the UK government.) He clearly felt that it was best to move on.

His war story is not the stuff of Hollywood legend. My dad never blew up a bridge or masterminded a daring prison escape. Yet he volunteered to fight the Japanese when he could have used his citizenship of a neutral country to escape the war. When the generals surrendered, he had to fight on – every day for three and a half years – just to stay alive. His torment lasted for 1,280 days. As a prisoner, he showed remarkable courage, resilience and tenacity in unbelievably inhumane conditions. He never gave up.

That is his biggest legacy. He was, and still is, my hero.

BIBLIOGRAPHY

BOOKS

Allister, W. (1995). *Where Life and Death Hold Hands*. Stoddart Publishing.

Barber, N. (1968). *Sinister Twilight*. Collins.

Bayly, C. & Harper, T. (2006). *Forgotten Wars: Freedom and Revolution in Southeast Asia*. Belknap Press.

Beattie, R. (2007). *The Thai–Burma Railway: The True Story of the Bridge on the River Kwai*. Asia Books.

Bell, P. M. H. (2012). *Twelve Turning Points of the Second World War*. Yale University Press.

Bix, H. P. (2000). *Hirohito and the Making of Modern Japan*. HarperCollins.

Bose, R. (2012). *Singapore at War: Secrets from the Fall, Liberation & Aftermath of WWII*. Marshall Cavendish Editions.

Boulle, P. (2012). *The Bridge on the River Kwai* (X. P. O. Denys, Trans.). Presidio Press. (Original work published 1952.)

Byrne, J. B. (2012). *Diary of War: World War II Memoirs of Lieutenant Colonel John Bernard Byrne*. Xlibris.

Chang, I. (1997). *The Rape of Nanking: The Forgotten Holocaust of World War II*. Basic Books.

Charles, H. R. (1988). *Last Man Out: Surviving the Burma–Thailand Death Railway*. Ballantine Books.

Chater, L. (2001). *Behind the Fence*. Vanwell Publishing.

Clavell, J. (1962). *King Rat*. Little, Brown and Company.

Coast, J. (1946). *Railroad of Death*. The Vanguard Press.

Daws, G. (1994). *Prisoners of the Japanese: POWs of World War II in the Pacific*. William Morrow and Company.

Dower, J. W. (2000). *Embracing Defeat: Japan in the Wake of World War II*. W. W. Norton & Company.

Dunlop, E. E. (1986). *The War Diaries of Weary Dunlop: Java and the Burma–Thailand Railway, 1942-1945*. Nelson.

Flanagan, R. (2013). *The Narrow Road to the Deep North*. Vintage Books.

Futamatsu, Y. (1987). *Across the Three Pagodas Pass: The Story of the Thai–Burma Railway*. Orchid Press.

Gordon, E. (2002). *To End All Wars*. Zondervan Publishing.

Hardie, R. (1983). *The Burma–Siam Railway: The Secret Diary of Dr. Robert Hardie, 1942–45*. Imperial War Museum.

Hastings, M. (2007). *Nemesis: The Battle for Japan, 1944–45*. HarperPress.

Henderson, S. (1987). *Comrades of the Kwai: The True Story of the British POWs Who Survived the Building of the Thai–Burma Railway*. Grafton Books.

Ishiguro, K. (1986). *An Artist of the Floating World*. Faber & Faber.

Jackson, B. (2016). *A Doctor's Sword: How an Irish Doctor Survived War, Captivity and the Atomic Bomb*. The Collins Press.

Keegan, J. (1987). *The Second World War*. Viking.

Kennedy, R. (1956). *Canton Chronicle*.

Kinvig, C. (1992). *River Kwai Railway: The Story of the Burma–Siam Railroad*. Brassey's.

Lomax, E. (1995). *The Railway Man*. W. W. Norton & Company.

MacCarthy, A. (1979). *A Doctor's War*. HarperCollins.

McArthur, B. (2005). *Surviving the Sword: Prisoners of the Japanese in the Far East, 1942–45*. Random House.

McIntosh, D. (1997). *Hell on Earth: Aging Faster, Dying Sooner*. McGraw-Hill.

O'Reilly, B., & Dugard, M. (2016). *Killing the Rising Sun: How America Vanquished World War II Japan.* Henry Holt & Co.

Owen, F. (1960). *The Fall of Singapore.* Penguin Books.

Owtram, H. C. (2017). *1000 Days on the River Kwai: The Secret Diary of a British camp Commandant.* Pen and Sword Military.

Parkin, R. (1965). *Into the Smother.* The Hogarth Press.

Pavillard, S. (1960). *Bamboo Doctor.* Macmillan & Co.

Rawlings, L. (1972). *And the Dawn Came Up Like Thunder: Autobiography of a POW.* William Kimber.

Reed, B. (1990). *Lost Souls of the River Kwai.* Pen and Sword Military.

Russell, L. (1958). *The Knights of Bushido.* Cassell.

Sakamoto, M. (2014). *Forgiveness.* HarperCollins.

Searle, R. (1986). *To the Kwai and Back: War Drawings 1939–1945.* Collins.

Stewart, J. (1988). *To the River Kwai: Two Journeys - 1943 and 1974.* Macmillan.

Summer, J. (2005). *The Colonel of Tamarkan.* HarperCollins.

Time-Life Books (1989). *History of the Second World War.* Time-Life Books.

Toland, J. (1970). *The Rising Sun: The Decline and Fall of the Japanese Empire, 1936-1945.* Random House.

Twigg, R. (2015). *Survivor on the River Kwai*. Penguin.

Urquhart, A. (2010). *The Forgotten Highlander*. Little, Brown.

Van der Post, L. (1971). *The Night of the New Moon*. Hogarth Press.

Velmans, L. (2003). *Long Way Back to the River Kwai*. Arcade Publishing.

Widders, R. (2011). *The Emperor's Irish Slaves*. The History Press.

INTERNET SOURCES

2/4th Machine Gun Battalion. https://2nd4thmgb.com.au

Anzac Portal. https://anzacportal.dva.gov.au

Australian War Memorial. https://awm.gov.au

Britain-at-war.org / Death Railway. https://www.britain-at-war.org.uk

Chesworth, Andrew. Planning and Realities: The Recovery of Britain's Far East Prisoners of War, 1941–1945. PhD Thesis, University of Sheffield. https://etheses.whiterose.ac.uk

Cribb, R. (2018). The Life and Trial of Cho Un-kuk, Korean War Criminal. *Critical Asian Studies*, 50 (3), 329–352. https://criticalasianstudies.org

Eldridge, Sears (Macalester College, Minnesota). Captive Audiences/Captive Performers: Music and Theatre as Strategies for Survival on the Thailand-Burma Railway 1942–1945. https://digitalcommons.macalester.edu

Far Eastern Heroes. https://www.far-eastern-heroes.org.uk

Far Eastern Prisoners of War Community. https://www.fepow-community.org.uk

Forces War Records. https://uk.forceswarrecords.com

Green Writing Room. https://greenwritingroom.com

Pavillard, S.S. Medical Experiences in Siam, *British Medical Journal*, 26 January 1946. https://www.bmj.com/content/1/4438/135

Prisoners of War of the Japanese 1942–1945. https://www.pows-of-japan.net

University of California, Berkeley War Crimes Studies Centre. https://www.ocf.berkeley.edu

ACKNOWLEDGEMENTS

For me, telling this amazing story has been a labour of love. My dream was that my parents' story would be remembered by future generations of our family. Now, I can realistically hope that many others will also enjoy learning about it. This could only have happened with the help of many wonderful people.

First and foremost, I'd like to thank my mother. She was a natural storyteller. After my father passed away, she was very happy to share his wartime stories, and memories of their life together. Without her there would be no book.

My family encouraged me every step of the way. Maggie as always gave her love and constant support. Deirdre contributed her technical abilities and typing skills. Irene provided a moving narrative of her visit to the

British National Museum. Mary Clare, Angie, Stephen and Aisling helped with editing suggestions. My siblings gave me their childhood memories. Dustin, Kate and Nancy, Aoife and Flo, James, Thea and Pia – your love inspired me to share the story. Finlay and Sadhbh showed me that future generations will treasure these wartime experiences. This was truly a team effort.

This journey would never have started without my passion for genealogy. In the early days, this was nurtured and developed by many family historians. This list is by no means complete, but I would like to acknowledge and thank Olive Dawson, Barbara Harding, Nicholas Ring, and the late Gerald Perry, Sr Barbara Kennedy and Michael Gleeson. You sowed the seed.

In more recent times, I've been ably assisted by many other people who were generous with their time and knowledge. In Canada, the insights of Patricia Mark and Jack Farr were invaluable. In Switzerland, researchers at the International Red Cross and Swiss National Archives tried hard to help. Ronnie Taylor, the administrator of the Far East Prisoners of War website, kindly gave me permission to use maps and first-hand accounts of camps on the Death Railway. You helped the story grow.

I must acknowledge the hard-working professionals at Gill Books. Patrick O'Donoghue recognised the importance of this unique story, and has steadily guided the project to a finish line. Isabelle Hanrahan has been a skilled, thoughtful and kind editor. Graham Thew designed an attractive cover. Many thanks to you all.

Finally, I want to remember my dad. Though you never wanted fame, I felt compelled to tell your story as best as I could. I hope my words have done you proud.